THE CONVERSION

by

S.L. HENDRICKSON

Bloomington, IN

authorHOUSE™

Milton Keynes, UK

AuthorHouse™
1663 Liberty Drive, Suite 200
Bloomington, IN 47403
www.authorhouse.com
Phone: 1-800-839-8640

AuthorHouse™ UK Ltd.
500 Avebury Boulevard
Central Milton Keynes, MK9 2BE
www.authorhouse.co.uk
Phone: 08001974150

First published by AuthorHouse 5/23/2006

ISBN: 1-4259-0986-8 (sc)

Printed in the United States of America
Bloomington, Indiana

This book is printed on acid-free paper.

I

The sun set was sending golden rays of light in to Marilyn's office. Streaks of light danced on the office walls. Marilyn turned around in her chair and looked out the window. Lately she had been spending more and more time watching the sunsets. When she first moved into the corner office it took her several weeks before she even noticed that the windows faced west. As the sun sank below the horizon the clouds turned a deep blue with yellow tops and the city lights shined more brightly.

Marilyn was feeling listless. It was getting increasing harder to concentrate. For the past few weeks she had felt that there was something missing in her life. As the sun disappeared the lights of the city made for a breathtaking view. She knew on the city streets below the people of the night would be coming out. Sometimes, after working very late, she would go walking and would marvel at the metamorphosis of the city. In the day it was filled limos and people in business suites, power brokers and their subordinates working on or chasing that next big deal. After sunset, all those people who made their living in the night would come out, deals consummated in the ally ways and the door ways. Sometimes, when she was extremely restless, she would go to the east side. She found it quite by accident when she had gotten off on the wrong subway stop. The hookers and pimps fascinated her. The way they talked and the clothes they wore. She would wonder what it would be like to wear the most revealing clothes and yell at cars as they drove by, wonder what it would be like to talk to man and make a deal for sex.

She would sometimes go into the bookstores and be intrigued and slightly aroused by all the different sexual material. She was always drawn to the magazines with pictures of female domination on the cover also fascinated by the different restraints and whips that hung behind the counter. She never bought anything, never went into the strip clubs or went in and watched any of the sex acts advertised on the outside of the clubs but she always wondered what it would be like to make your living performing sexual acts. She was never hassled on these little excursions, everyone could tell from her appearance she was an uptown woman. That was as close as she every got to carnal knowledge.

She thought about going home but it was such a long train ride. The town house she bought in the suburbs was to satisfy her mother who thought the inner city was too dangerous. The house was an excellent tax deduction but not very practical since she was working twelve to fourteen hours a day so she had taken to sleeping on the large leather couch, turning her office into a make shift apartment.

Marilyn turned around and looked at the three computer screens on her desk. They all contained data on the latest billion-dollar merger. Marilyn and her ten member staff had been going over the financial records of one the world's biggest corporations for weeks. She fed on the power and responsibility like a drug. It had kept her high for years and she loved the many perks of the job, the six figure income, the limos, the private planes, the private parties but now she was losing enthusiasm and didn't know why. She looked at the small picture of her sister and her family that she kept on her desk. She never had any interest in marriage or a family. She may have sacrificed family and relationships but she was proud of what she had accomplished; top of her class at Harvard and one of the ten most influential people on Wall Street. Her recommendation could approve or kill a billion dollar merger sending a companies stock up or down. She had access to the personal data on every company employee from the chairman of the board to the mail clerks. But lately, it was hard to focus on the simplest of tasks. She was only two months from turning forty. There was no time for a mid life crisis.

Marilyn sighed as got up and went into her private bathroom. She ran some cold water, got a wash cloth, held it under the water and then dabbed her face. She looked into the mirror. With the right make up she could be somewhat good looking but now with the big bags under her eyes, the pale skin, the black, short cut, estranged hair, she thought her manly features made her look like an old hag.

A professional did her hair and makeup every week even though she always thought it was a waste of money because she wanted to make it with brains and not looks.

She took off her suite jacket and blouse, wet the washcloth and wiped under her arms. She took off her bra and looked at her breasts. They were tiny, no more than slight bumps on her chest but her nipples were large and dark. She had never thought of herself as attractive sexually and never cared. She was over six feet and all though both grade school and high school she was taller than most of the boys. They called her the 'stick'. She turned sideways and viewed her profile. She had a killer ass. It was large for her frame but it was firm and perfectly shaped. She had heard men make comments especially when she wore a tight skirt or pants suite. She ran her hands down her sides. Her ribs protruded slightly. Her stomach was still flat, still had an athletic body even though most of the time she was glued to a desk.

She ran one hand through her bush as she used her thumb to rub her nipple. She never touched herself sexually, not because she thought it was wrong or dirty, but because she was never interested. Now she was wondering why she was standing in the bathroom and touching herself. She got the washcloth wet with really cold water and then dabbed her face. She was really starting to wonder if she had gone off the deep end when her cell phone rang.

"Dam," Marilyn said as she scrambled to find her phone in the suite coat.

"Hello,"

"What are you doing kid, are you at the office, of course you're at the office. Have you had any supper yet?"

Marilyn picked up her blouse and covered her chest as if she could see her through the phone. It was Patricia, her best friend since college and one of the top attorneys in the city.

"I'm not doing anything," Marilyn said defensively. It almost felt like that time her mother caught her in the bathroom exploring herself.

"What, are you alright?"

"I'm fine."

"Well, if you haven't eaten then meet me at Cittais?"

"Ok, I will meet you there."

Marilyn put the phone down and using her middle finger touched herself. It was completely dry. She couldn't remember the last time it was really wet down there or excited. As she put back on her clothes she tried to remember the last time she had sex. It was almost three years ago at a conference for corporate tax accounting. She had met him at the bar, had too much to drink and could not remember if she enjoyed it or much of the details. It was the pattern that started in high school, get intoxicated, let them do what they wanted, forget about it as soon as possible, never thinking of her own needs or satisfaction. There had been only two sexual experiences in high school and one he never really penetrated her, not knowing what to do with a virgin and once in college with Patricia. Could that be what was missing? Is it sex, she thought but then she let it slip from her mind, got dressed, and shut down the computers.

II

The maître d' escorted her to Patricia's table. A good looking young man in a white shirt and tie came over and gave her a menu and took their drink order. Marilyn ordered a double scotch, neat. Patricia checked him out as he left. Marilyn just shook her head.

"When you quite looking, you quit living," Patricia said.

"You're incorrigible. You always were," Marilyn responded.

"And you look like hell."

"Thanks."

The waiter brought their drinks. "Are we ready to order Miss?"

Marilyn ordered the ravioli and Patricia ordered the Alfredo. Patricia raised her eyebrows and pursed her lips as the waiter left.

"Now there is a nice piece of boy candy."

"You're old enough to be his mother."

Patricia was a year older than Marilyn and had also given up family and relationships for her career. Her blonde hair was short and shaggy and she didn't wear any makeup. Her job was to put bad guys in jail, to deal with the dregs of society so she never cared about her personal appearance. She was still good looking and knew it. She was well endowed and Marilyn always wondered what it was like to carry around those massive things all the time.

"I don't know how you keep it all together?" Marilyn asked after draining most of her drink.

"What do you mean?"

"You always seem so vibrant. You never seem to get run down."

"That's because I make sure that I take care of my personal needs on a regular basis."

"What do you mean?"

"I am talking about that thing between your legs."

Marilyn felt her face become red and felt even more uncomfortable when she noticed the waiter, afraid that he had heard them.

"Do you want another drink, Miss?"

"Please," Marilyn responded.

"I know you have always been uptight sexually," Patricia responded after the waiter walked away. It was true. Marilyn had always been the bookworm, the class valedictorian; the tall, awkward girl, never asked out on dates, never hung out with the popular girls. She spent her time in high school and college buried in her studies.

"If you take care of that on a regular basis, it makes all the difference in the world."

It was late and way past the normal supper hour. There were only a couple of business men on the other side of the restaurant but Marilyn still felt uncomfortable talking about such things in a public place.

"Who has time for relationships," Marilyn responded as the waiter brought her drink.

"I am not talking about relationships. I know who needs it, all that who is going to call who, dealing with parents and relatives, worrying about what to buy on birthdays and holidays. I'm talking about dealing with it on a professional level."

Marilyn just shook her head; totally confused.

"You have your clothes done by a professional."

"Yes."

"You have your hair and nails done by professionals and I'm sure you have your car done by a professional so why not have your sexual needs taken care of by professionals."

Marilyn discovered she was famished, was busy eating and was only half hearing what Patricia was saying.

"You mean a gigolo?" Marilyn giggled as the half finished second drink started to hit her.

"No, not exactly, here I am going to do you a favor." Patricia unzipped her portfolio and took out her day planner. She went through her business card holder and pulled out a card. She wrote her name on the back of the card and handed it to Marilyn. She was really starting

6

to fee the effects of the drinks and almost dropped it on her plate. On the card was AVALON: Personal Services. There was a phone number underneath the gold lettering but no address.

"What's this?" Marilyn asked.

"Just give them a call and set up an appointment. It's very exclusive. You have to be recommended by someone. It will change your life."

Marilyn slid it into her day planner and forgot about it just as quickly.

By the time they walked out of the restaurant, Patricia was half carrying Marilyn. The street was deserted. The lit skyscrapers towered around them. Patricia waved at a cab. It moved over one lane and then the off duty light came on.

"Basted cabbies, Patricia yelled, "What, you don't want to deal with a couple of drunk, white women?" They both laughed hysterically.

Marilyn was wobbling on her high heels.

"How many drinks, did you have any way, I better get you home and into bed."

"No, I have a ton of work to do. I need to go back to the office."

Patricia waved at another cab and this one stopped, they both fell into the back seat.

"Grayson office plaza," Patricia said. The cabby grunted something.

Marilyn's skirt had bunched up when she got in reveling, a good part of her thigh. Patricia put her hand on her thigh and then worked her hand up to her inner thigh. She massaged her leg. Marilyn was wondering why she had not put back on her panty hose. Patricia put her hand between her legs and rested it on the flesh protruding through her panties.

"I can help you down there if you want me to?"

Marilyn put her head on her shoulder and thought about that time in college. They had been roommates for almost a year. Marilyn had gotten accustomed to seeing Patricia run around half dressed. They were the odd couple. Marilyn was thin, sexless, and always covered herself from head to toe with sweat pants and sweat shirts even when she slept. Patricia was full figured and spent a lot of time running around in just a bra and panties or in a nightgown that hid almost nothing. One day Marilyn was taking a shower and Patricia just pulled back the shower curtain and stepped in. Marilyn was shocked. She just stood there, frozen; she didn't know what to say. Patricia took the soap and slowly started to run the soap over her body. She ran the soap over the top of her chest, down each arm, and over her flat stomach. Then she ran the soap over her own massive breasts and over her protruding nipples. Marilyn just stared at her breasts and thinking how beautiful they were, large, firm, the pink nipples sticking straight up. Patricia stepped into Marilyn and ran soap down her back. Marilyn grew tense. She was not use to feeling another person's hands on her body. Patricia lathered her back and then ran the soap over her ass. Then she ran her fingers between her ass cheeks.

"You have a nice ass."

Patricia massaged her ass for a few moments and then tried to get her hands between her legs but Marilyn kept her legs tightly together. Patricia ran the soap over her stomach and then put the soap in to her hand. She guided her hand between her legs.

"Wash me."

Marilyn ran the soap all over her bush and then between her legs. Patricia titled her head back and closed her eyes as Marilyn washed her flabby thighs. Patricia pulled her in close and raked her fingernails gently over her back and ass. Marilyn felt herself melt into her as she continued to run her hand over her bush and between her legs but never touching that most sensitive spot. Patricia adjusted the spray so it rinsed them off and then adjusted it so the water ran between her breasts. She pushed her breasts together and the water ran between them like a river. Marilyn just stared at the water cascading down her breasts and thinking it was the most erotic thing she had ever seen. Patricia lifted them, offering them to her.

"I know you want them."

Marilyn kissed the top of her breast and then down the massive globe until she came to her nipple. She sucked it in. Marilyn could not believe how stiff it was. Her own nipples had never been like that. She liked the way it moved and tasted as she ran her tongue over it. When it slipped from her mouth, she looked up at Patricia and felt embarrassed. She covered up her own little tits with her arms as she got out of the shower. Patricia followed her out and even though Marilyn was much taller grabbed her around the waist and pulled her back and then reaching around and pushing her hand between her legs. Marilyn had never like talking about her sex life so Patricia had no idea about her lack of experience.

"I can't," Marilyn said as she tensed up.

"Why, because I'm a woman?"

"I don't know how."

"I will show you."

Marilyn was just about to break away when she felt fingers going between her ass cheeks. She stopped and held still, perfectly still; afraid the felling was going to stop. Patricia ran her fingers up and down between her cheeks and then found her clit with the other hand.

"Just let me please you and then I will show you how to please me."

Patricia massaged her whole ass as she took her index finger and moved it lightly in a circular motion on her clit. She increased the pressure on her clit and Marilyn finally spread her legs apart. Patricia drove her fingers between her cheeks as she slipped a finger inside. Marilyn moaned at the invasion. Patricia stopped.

"I'm sorry. I had no idea you were still a virgin.

"Please don't stop. "

She could barely get the tip of one finger inside as she bent down and ran her tongue between her ass cheeks. Marilyn loved the feeling of something warm and wet between her cheeks. Suddenly she felt something building deep within her. It was building and feeling like it was pushing up through her.

"No, no, stop," Marilyn said as she tensed up.

"You're going to have an orgasm, just let it happen," Patricia replied.

Marilyn's mind started to race. She had never felt anything like this. It felt like she was going to explode from the inside. Marilyn remembered what her mother had told her about how only a man gets sexual pleasure and that was the cross women had to bear and that thought made the pressure subsided but she felt just a small gush of fluid inside. Patricia took her by the hand and led into her bedroom.

She sat on the bed and spread legs wide. Marilyn had no idea what to do.

"Just kiss it," Patricia said.

Marilyn got on her knees and she thought it would be disgusting but it wasn't. After a few light kisses, Marilyn was running her tongue up and down liking the taste and smell of her womanhood. Patricia moaned and then lifted up her tit and sucked on her own nipple. She moved her hips forward trying to get more of Marilyn's tongue inside of her but she was just barely penetrating her so she sucked on her nipple harder and used her other hand to massage her own clit. In a few moments, she was shaking as an orgasm racked her body and her breathing was labored.

"Thanks, I needed that."

Marilyn quickly got dressed. They never did it again and never talked about it.

The cab pulled up to building. Patricia gave the cabby a big tip. They both straightened up their clothes before going into the lobby. Marilyn explained to the security guard that she would probable be working through the night and that Patricia would be down shortly. As soon as they got inside Marilyn's office Patricia grabbed her hand that was headed for the light switch.

"Keep the lights off." The other office towers made the office glow with reflective light. Patricia pulled her close, reached up underneath her blouse, finding her bare breast. She found her nipple and tugged at it.

"I want you."

Marilyn had just enough liquor not to care. Patricia led her over to the big leather couch that had been her bed so many nights. Marilyn flopped on the couch and Patricia kicked off her shoe and got between her legs. She grabbed her skirt and pulled it down over her hips almost breaking the zipper, pulled the panties down her long, white legs.

"You're so skinny but you're so hot," Patricia said and then buried her face between her legs. Marilyn put her head on the back of couch and thought if she got a few hours sleep she still could run her reports early enough in the morning before the rest of her staff arrived and could be back on schedule by mid morning. Patricia drove her tongue in as far as she could and moved it from side to side but she remained dry and lifeless. Marilyn felt very warm so she unbuttoned her blouse and then Patricia went up and sucked hard on her nipples. She pulled on it with her teeth until it was hard and firm. She sucked on the other nipple as she worked the other between her thumb and forefinger. In a few moments her nipples were engorged.

"Your nipples are so dam big." They were very dark, almost black. Patricia continued to tongue her nipples as she took off her own suite jacket and blouse. The lacy, white material barley contained her tanned mounds. Marilyn looked down at her ample cleavage and had a sudden urge to bury her face in it. Patricia went back down between her legs trying again to bring it to life. Marilyn stuck her hand between Patricia's breasts and wondered if anything else could fee so soft and warm. She pulled down her bra straps and pushed the cups down over her tits. She massaged both of them and raked her fingernails over her nipples. Patricia rewarded her by really going after her, holding nothing back until her face was all wet but Marilyn barely noticed.

Patricia stood up and took off her skirt, pantyhose, and slid down her sopping, wet panties.

"Lay down," Patricia demanded. Patricia straddled her head and lowered herself onto her mouth. "Now eat me, I want to get off."

Marilyn moved her tongue around but she still had no idea of what to do. At that moment she just wanted to go to sleep so she could get up in the morning and start working. Patricia moved around on her face, covering it with her fluid.

"Eat me," Patricia said as she grabbed her hair and lifted her head up and Marilyn was wondering why she would get pleasure from this. She moved her tongue around more forcefully hoping it would end soon.

"Oh yea, that's it baby, eat my hot, box." But Marilyn quite so Patricia raked herself over her chin and nose, up and down and side to side. Her large, flabby thighs were beating the sides of Marilyn's head. Suddenly Patricia stopped and the last thing Marilyn remembered was her face being bathed in warm juice.

III

Marilyn awoke to her assistant, Jason, standing over her.

"Want some coffee?" he asked. Marilyn could not remember getting dressed but was thankful that she wasn't half naked.

"Another late night?"

"Yes, very late."

Jason handed her a cup of coffee. "The San Diego office is calling, they want those

income projections by noon and corporate called and they want the five year tax outlays before the end of business today."

"No problem," Marilyn responded as she pushed the events of last night quickly out of her mind. In a few minutes, she was up to full speed, planning the activities for the day in her mind and giving her staff their duties.

Marilyn spent the next three nights sleeping on the office couch. She would lay down on the large, over stuffed, leather couch with her lap top until she couldn't hold her eyes open and then sleep a few hours and start all over again. Although she put in the time, it still felt like she was just going through the motions. The drive that had pushed her through high school and college was waning. There was a void in her life.

All that week she avoided Patricia's phone calls. On Thursday, she went down to the east side of town and walked through the bookstores. She was almost at the counter with a magazine that featured a woman on the cover dressed in platform heels, fish net stockings, a corset, and holding a whip as she straddled a man on all fours tethered by a leash, but she was scared off by loud couple at the counter.

On Friday she was updating her day planner when she noticed the card Patricia gave her.

She looked at it for several moments and then surprised herself when she dialed the number.

"Avalon, personal services, how may I help you."

Marilyn was silent.

"May I help you?"

"I would like to make an appointment."

"And your name, please."

"Marilyn Stokke."

She heard typing and then the woman on the other end said, "This will this be your first appointment with us?"

"Yes."

"We have an opening at ten on Saturday."

"You are open on Saturday?"

"Yes, we are open seven days a week."

Marilyn wrote down the address surprised that it was uptown just assuming it would be in the sleazy part of town somewhere between the tattoo parlors and erotic book stores. She was surprised again at their office. The lobby was lavishly furnished much like her own. There were plants and paintings on the wall. She didn't know exactly what she expected but it was more in line with one of those bath house, massage parlors she saw down on the east side. There name and company logo with New York, London, and Paris in shinny steel letters hung above a large receptionist desk made of dark, well polished wood.

"May I help you?" asked the receptionist.

"My name is Marilyn Stokke. I have an appointment.

"Yes, please be seated, some one will be right out."

The only other person in the lobby was a man, in an expensive suite, entering data into his Palm Pilot. Marilyn no more than sat down when a woman, about her own age, came out. She was dressed in a burgundy business suite, with a coral colored, ruffled blouse. Her hair was combed back and tied tightly. Marilyn figured her outfit was more expensive than her own and she made a mental note to ask her where she bought her clothes.

"I'm sorry if you have been waiting."

"No, actually I just arrived." They shook hands.

"I know how busy our clients are so I don't like to keep them waiting. Do you have our card?" Marilyn handed it to her. She turned it over. "Oh yes, Patricia Hurling, she is one of our best clients, please come with me."

Marilyn followed her into the inner office, down a hallway, and then into a small conference room. There was small, highly polished conference table and several chairs. The office over looked the river. Marilyn felt like she was in a very professional office.

"Please be seated, my name is Leslie Borden, I am a licensed sexual therapist."

Marilyn could not help but snicker a little inside. She had never heard of a licensed sexual therapist. It was a fancy title for something not unlike her own title of senior, vice president of accounting and corporate mergers. Leslie sat down, her back straight, her hands folded neatly on the table.

"And what service can we provide for you."

"What services do you provide?" Marilyn replied trying not to sound sarcastic.

"Our services are tailored to each individual." She opened up her leather bound valise. "I see here that you are an accountant." Marilyn was just wondering how she knew that when Leslie added, "We do a complete background check on all of our perspective clients."

"Yes."

"Then I will bottom line it for you. Our job is to help our clients achieve sexual satisfaction. That may take on the form of counseling both mental and physically, providing role playing, or providing devices that enhance the sexual experience. We also provide, in some rare cases, medical procedures to correct defects or provide implants. Or we may provide environments that help the client achieve their sexual satisfaction. So, what service most interests you?"

"I'm really not sure," Marilyn said and hoping she didn't sound flippant because she was defiantly intrigued.

"Perhaps if I ask you a few questions we will get an idea of where our starting point is and then develop a plan of action. Have you ever had an orgasm?"

Marilyn was silent. She was totally unsure.

"If you have to think about it then the answer is probable no. Have you ever had a gratifying sexual experience?" again Marilyn was silent. She wrote no on her pad.

Do you think sex is wrong or dirty?"

"Defiantly not," Marilyn said quickly.

"Did you parents have a satisfying sex life?"

"I'm not sure."

"Did your mother ever tell you that a woman's orgasm was a myth or not important?"

"She said that they just didn't happen and it was our cross to bear."

Leslie shut her notebook. "I have been doing this for over ten years and I have seen many women like yourself, so please don't feel like you are alone. The woman's orgasm is not a myth and it is a beautiful experience. It is a natural biological function. Look at it as nature's compensation for the pain of pregnancy and child birth. It is achieved by both mental and physical stimulus. In fact, in that way men and woman are the same because it takes both mental and physical stimulus to reach an orgasm. For men it is more physical than mental but the mental is still important. Men are more responsive to stimuli by sight so that is why they prefer strip clubs, movies, and magazines. For woman it is mental foreplay that is more important but even though physical contact is less important for the woman than for the man proper techniques can greatly enhance the pleasure. I would recommend that you have a brief examination by one of our doctors to rule out and physical reason why you may not be able to achieve an orgasm. Then I recommend one of our mental evaluations to determine your mental triggers, or to put it more simply to determine what really turns you on. Do you have a casual or steady partner?"

"No."

"Then I recommend seeing one of our clinical therapists who will show you how to have an orgasm by yourself."

"I don't know, it sounds like a lot things to do and what is the cost."

Leslie smiled, "I can see why you are an accountant. The person who recommended you pays the first visit. If you want to continue with our services you can be billed monthly, quarterly, or yearly and we accept all major credit cards. Of course you will never have to pay for a service that you are not completely satisfied with."

"I don't know a thing about your company."

"We are a fortune five hundred company and traded on New York Stock Exchange. We have been in business for over fifteen years. Our clients included corporate executives, politicians, and people in the entertainment field. Our client list, and the services we provide, is kept completely confidential, as yours will be. In all the time that I have worked here I have never received a complaint about our service or our fees. It will only take a few hours. I hope Marilyn," Leslie said as she stood up, "that by the time you leave here today you will have had the first sexually satisfying experience of your life."

Marilyn was more intrigued than anything else. She half expected this to be some type of elaborate joke, couldn't imagine people, successful people, paying to be sexually satisfied. Why would they? She thought. Marilyn shook her hand and then followed her to an elevator and they went down three levels. She was led into a doctor's office "I will leave you in the staff's capable hands," Leslie said as a nurse came into the office. First she completed a sexual survey, in record time. There was little to tell. When it came to the part that asked about her sexual preferences she left all the questions blank. One question asked if she preferred men or women or both. She marked men because she didn't think what she did with Patricia really counted.

"Please get undressed," the nurse said as she handed her a medical gown. "The doctor will be right with you. As she got undressed she noticed the medical diploma on the wall. Harvard Medical School, very impressive, Marilyn thought.

"Good morning, I'm Doctor Fisher, how are we feeling today?"

"Fine."

She looked at her folder. She was an older woman with Asian features but no accent.

"Are you on any regular medications?"

"No."

"Do you drink or do drugs on a daily basis."

"No, of course not just the social drink now and then."

"In general is your health good?"

"Yes."

She wrote everything down on the chart.

"Fine, let's see what we have then."

She washed her hands. They made small talk about being alumnus of Harvard as she checked her heart, breathing, and reflexes. She lay down on the examination table and she put her feet in the stirrups. It was just like her other examinations until she placed her thumb on her clit and pushed down.

"Is it sensitive there?"

"Yes."

The doctor ran her fingers over her private parts, not in a sexual way, but in a purely medical way.

"Is it sensitive there?"

"Yes,"

"Well, I would say you are in perfect health. Just relax and I will send in the therapist."

Outside the room she handed the chart to a therapist. "For all intents and purposes we have a virgin. She is perfect healthy but I would say she has never had any meaningful penetration."

"Thank you doctor," she replied taking the chart. She looked at it a few moments and then told the nurse to move the client to sexual, therapy room. Marilyn found herself in a room that was just the opposite of the sterile examination room. The lights were very dim. There was a projection screen on one wall. The walls and ceiling were a dark blue. There were various cabinets around the room and in the center of the room was a padded, brown, leather chair, the kind you would find in the more expensive dentist offices that could be adjusted to multiple positions. Marilyn settled into the chair and she liked the way the cool leather felt against her skin.

In a few moments a young girl came in wearing a nurse's uniform with buttons down the front that looked like they were ready to pop. Marilyn noticed she had the kind of body that men would drool over. Men would say that she was really built. She sat on stool and slid it over to the table.

"My name is Kim; I'm a sexual therapist if you prefer a man that could be arranged."

"No, that's fine."

Just then Leslie came in. "I would like to take care of Miss Stokke, personally, if you don't mind.

"Of course not," Kim replied and then left the room.

"I hope you don't mind Marilyn but I have a lot more experience in dealing with woman with sexual dysfunctions than Kim does."

"I guess so." Marilyn never thought she had a sexual dysfunction.

"Don't take this the wrong way but it not very often we run across a woman of your age with such limited sexual experience." "Have you ever given yourself an orgasm?"

"No," Marilyn replied defensively, deep down she still didn't think it was a natural thing.

Leslie took off her suite coat jacket and then unbuttoned the top two buttons of her blouse. She then massaged the back of Marilyn's legs.

"Just relax. Just think you are going to get a very good massage." Marilyn had several massages on the corporate junkets and had always enjoyed them. She didn't care if a man did it or a woman they could almost put her to sleep. Leslie took Marilyn's hand and put her first to fingers together and guided them to her clit.

"I want you to move your finger in a circular motion, that's it like that," she said as she guided her fingers. "Now press down while you move your fingers." Leslie slid a finger up and down but she was completely dry.

"It helps if you think of something sexual, someone you had sex with before or would like to have sex. I always think of Brad Pitt myself."

That made Marilyn giggle but she couldn't think of anything. She only a few sexual thoughts her entire life and she always put them out of her mind as quickly as possible. Leslie checked and she was still completely dry.

"Here let's remove your gown."

"Sometimes it helps if someone else does it the first time." Leslie put her fingers on her clit and moved them one-way and then the other.

"Try and think of something that really turns you on."

Suddenly it just popped into her mind. She had never thought of it before but she imagined walking into a barn full of stalls and in each stall was a man she had been interested in tethered by a leather strap. She was wearing fish net stockings, a bustier that pushed up her breasts and she was carrying a whip. They were all shouting and begging to let them please her. She cracked the whip and they became silent. Leslie fingers were flying over her clit as took her other hand and inserted her finger finding her wetness. Her finger went up and down and side to side and trying to push inside, trying to open her up. Marilyn was starting to sweat and her breathing was a little rapid. She felt that pressure deep inside as she opened the door of the first stall and a dark haired boy was on his knees, the boy that made out with her but had stopped short of doing anything. She towered over him. His hands were tied behind his back and the leather strap around his neck was tied to a post that kept him from reaching her. Marilyn stepped closer and he cowered before her. She moved closer, spread her legs and stood over him. He lapped at her as she brought the whip down on his back and ass.

The pressure was building more and more and she thought she was going to explode. "Please stop," as she tried to push Leslie's hand away from her clit.

"I'm not going to stop. It's perfectly natural and you are going to love it when it happens."

And it did happen as the boy serviced her and she brought the whip down on him. A flood of warm juice flowed through her and a wave went through her, starting down deep inside, flowing though her whole body, and then she floated like she was on a cloud. It was the biggest, most intense, release she had ever felt in her life. She could hear and feel Leslie sucking in her juice as it flowed out of her.

She did it for what Marilyn thought was an eternity.

"Sorry, that was not very professional of me, but I've never had a virgin before. You just had your first orgasm."

"Is that what men feel when they come."

"Yes, but about thousand times stronger."

"Those lucky basterds."

"A man can come only once or twice at the most at one time but a woman can have many orgasms. Would you like to feel it again, would like to learn how to do it yourself."

"Yes, yes I want to learn." Marilyn was almost begging. She really wanted to learn. She wanted to feel it again.

This time Leslie had her complete attention. She followed her instructions to the letter, rubbing her clit with her index and middle finger, varying the movement and pressure. Then she slipped a finger into her canal feeling her own wetness and then in and out per Leslie's instructions. There was a steady flow of juice now running out and onto the leather chair and Marilyn liked the warm, wet felling as the juice went between her ass and the chair. She was back in the stable again. In the next stall was the man from the convention panting and begging to please her. She whipped his back and ass and then she got on all fours and he mounted her, driving into her, as her next orgasm racked her body. In the next stall was Jason, laying on his back, naked, his legs and neck tethered by leather straps. It was so strange. She had never even thought of him in a sexual way because she just assumed he was gay but now he was naked and begging to please her. Marilyn straddled him and then lowered herself, telling him to please her. Her fingers were now working feverously on her clit as Leslie buried her head between her legs and Marilyn had never felt that much passion before.

After what seemed like hours, Leslie kissed her stomach and then kissed her way up to her nipple and Marilyn was disappointed because she wanted more of that passion between her legs but when Leslie took her nipple into her mouth she wanted her there too.

Marilyn closed her eyes and floated again and when she opened her eyes and saw her nipple between Leslie's full lips she thought it was the sexiest thing she had ever seen. She jumped a little when Leslie's teeth grazed the nipple. She had never thought her nipples could get that hard or be that sensitive. Marilyn closed her eyes as Leslie sucked on one nipple and squeezed the other between her fingers. Now she was back in the stable and Jason has his tongue deep inside of her as she ran her hand up and down his shaft. She imagined his shaft to be long and thin but when she slid down on it she thought it filled her completely and as Leslie gave her more passion between her legs she felt that pressure build deep inside but this time she welcomed it and couldn't wait for it to rush through her. She whipped Jason's chest and told him that he would be beaten severely if he did not please her. Leslie had her middle finger buried inside to the knuckle as another wave went through her body giving her that total release again and more juice flowed between her ass and the chair. Leslie was drinking as much as she could. Marilyn closed her eyes and relaxed and was back in the stable bucking against Jason's hardness, whipping his inner thighs, and bouncing up and down on his shaft. Another wave came again, quicker, but not as intense, and as she floated, she knew now why Patricia and some of the other girls in high school and college were such sluts.

"Did you enjoy it?" Leslie asked.

"Yes, it was incredible. I never knew it was like that."

Leslie drew some water in a bowl and got a sponge. She wiped off her forehead and then ran the sponge down her arms and across her breasts.

"You have a wonderful service here," Marilyn said, closed her eyes, and started floating again.

"You could use our service every week at this time if you like," Leslie responded as she wiped off her stomach and inner thighs in a very sexual way.

Marilyn signed up for one more visit before she left. She went straight home, went into the bathroom, stripped, and examined herself. Her nipples were still stiff. She closed her eyes and took her nipple between her finger and thumb. She massaged her clit and was in the stable again. She was in a chair that was above the dozen men that knelt before her. She pointed to a young blond man and summoned him. He came to her and then drove into her. He pumped in and out of her as she guided him to her nipple. He sucked greedily on it. In a few moments, Marilyn's felt another explosion and her juice sprayed against her thighs. It was not a fluke, she thought.

Marilyn poured in her favorite soap and then filled the tub with hot water. The silky water caressed her. She ran the sponge down her arms and then down her long legs. It felt like every pour had come alive like her body had been an empty husk but now it had been awakened and fully alive. She ran the sponge over her chest and her hard nipples.

They had been hard for the longest time. She lay motionless and let the bubbles float around her, laid her head back, and her mind started to race. She was on her way to becoming a sensual being. She wanted Leslie again, wanted Patricia to service her. She reached down and found her clit and massaged it with two fingers just how Leslie had showed her but it had to be wrong to have another orgasm she thought to have that many in one day had to be wrong, maybe she had gone to far, but at that moment she just didn't care, for the first time in her life, did something just because it fell good. She made a mental note to ask Patricia how many times she had pleased herself in one day.

Marilyn usually wore full length pajamas or sweat pants and a sweat shirt to bed but for the first time since she was a teenager crawled into bed completely naked and right before she fell asleep she wondered what it would feel like to have a man really service her.

IV

Marilyn was sipping coffee, and looking at her day planner. Sunday was always the day to plan the activities of the next week, jot down daily goals in the margin for each day and cross-reference to the monthly goals. Then she would make notes in the hourly markings for each day, but now, she had no interest in it. Finally she closed it and went into the bedroom. It took a few minutes to find the two boxes in the back of her closet. She put them on the bed. The tops were covered with dust. She took out the articles of clothing one at a time and held them up. Some she had not worn since college, others, not since high school. She found a red, mini skirt. She took off her robe, stepped into it, got it up over her hips, but she couldn't get the zipper closed. She had worn it only once when she tried to fit in with the other girls by going to the mall and hoping some boy would notice but the boys just teased her about how tall she was. In the bottom of the second box, was the outfit she wore at junior prom. She went to the prom alone and stayed for a couple of hours before going home in a state of rejection. She never attended the senior prom. She held up the little dress by its thin straps. It was light blue with a plunging neckline and backless. She found the white garter belt and white nylons and put them on. She put on the dress and it came down to mid thigh and it was very tight. The material gathered between her legs. The high hells tightened up her legs. She modeled the outfit in front of the mirror. I look just like a hooker, she thought. Then remembered the deceivers she used in high school, folded up tissue stuck into the bra, filling it out. She looked at herself in the mirror and then fell on the bed wondering if she had gone over the deep end, actually contemplating being a hooker. It was wicked and dangerous and it excited her. There was a throbbing between her legs and she wanted to have another orgasm but it had to be wrong to have so many. Her mind started racing. The cab would drop her off where she had seen the hookers hanging out. Her hair was combed straight back, dark eye shadow and the red lip stick which was a stark contrast to her pale skin. She took up a position near a couple of women standing in a doorway as two black women were coming doing the sidewalk. Marilyn's heart was racing.

"Who are you and what are doing on my street? The black woman said with the large breasts and large ass who was wearing tight, orange, shorts that matched the color of her hair. The other black woman was smaller but with huge breasts that bulged out the top of the tight, one-piece dress.

"Who sent you down her, was it Darin? She continued with out taking hardly a breath. "If it was Darin, I'm going to have to cut that boy because this is my street and I don't need no skinny, white woman coming down here taking food away from my babies."

Marilyn did not know what to say at first. She had stood toe to toe with corporate raiders and high priced lawyers and had held her own but this was foreign territory.

"Oh, give it a rest, it's a free country," the older woman replied from the doorway.

"Honey, there's nothing in this world that's free especially this," she replied, grabbing her crotch.

"I don't think that I am any real competition, I just make you look better," Marilyn finally replied.

The black woman started to laugh. "You got that right girl. No man wants a skinny ass white woman when the can have this." She shook her large ass at Marilyn.

A stretch limo pulled up and the black tinted window went down. After a few moments the two black women got in and it pulled away.

"You're lucky they left there could have been trouble," the older woman said as she came over and offered Marilyn a cigarette.

"No, thank you." Her father had made her take defense classes so she could hold her own.

"You look like an uptown girl whose playing downtown." Marilyn new she would be out of her element. The woman was in her early forties with a voluptuous body.

"I bet she's from the suburbs and she's got herself a habit," the younger woman said from the doorway. She was in her early twenties, thin, but with large breasts.

"Is that it honey, have you got yourself a habit and need some money?"

"I'm just looking for some action."

"Well, you be careful. A lady can get hurt down here."

"Yea, don't let them smack you around it's not worth it," the younger one replied.

A dark sedan pulled up and the side window rolled down. The older woman walked over and bent over giving the driver a very good view of her ample cleavage.

"What do you charge," he asked.

"It's one hundred for a quickie or twenty five for a blow job."

The driver noticed Marilyn. "What about her?"

"You don't want her honey; she doesn't have the experience I can give you."

"She looks fresh, tell her to come over."

"He wants you honey."

Marilyn walked to the car.

Her heart was racing again as she massaged her clit very gently. She wanted it to be slow this time. She wanted to see how long she could make it last.

"How much?"

Marilyn boldly opened up the door and got in and crossed her long legs.

"You sure are tall."

"Do you like tall women?"

"I've never had a tall woman so how much?"

"What do you usually pay?" He was the kind of man she figured would pay for a woman. His dark hair was greasy looking and combed straight back. He had a large, gold chain around his neck. The top two buttons of his flowered shirt were unbuttoned exposing his hairy chest. He wasn't that bad looking and his small potbelly hanging over his polyester pants wasn't to disgusting.

"A hundred."

"For you honey, it's only fifty," she said rubbing his leg.

"Where to?"

"The Ambassador," It was sleazy looking motel she had seen from the train. When they arrived he wanted to pay for an hour but she talked him into paying for the night. She was now on more familiar ground, negotiating.

As soon as they entered the room he grabbed her ass.

"You've got a nice ass."

He pulled a bottle of whisky from his back pocket.

"No liquor," she said.

"Hey honey I'm paying for this."

Marilyn sat on the bed and spread her legs wide, showing him that she wasn't wearing any panties.

"Do me good and I will let you have it for free?"

He put the whisky on the dresser and got undressed as fast as he could.

Marilyn stood up; she was several inches taller than him. She unzipped her dress and let it fall. She undid her bra and let it fall.

"Man, you got some small tits."

"If you wanted big ones you should have taken one of the other women, besides I'm a virgin," she replied, still negotiating.

She could feel the bed was getting wet.

"Come on baby." She could never say the F- word, not out loud and not even now in her head so she said, "Do me".

He took off shorts. He was average size. Having only seen two her whole entire life she had no idea of the diversity in size and length.

He bent down to kiss her but she pushed him away.

"I don't need the foreplay just do me."

"All right baby, that's what I like to hear."

He poked around for a few moments and then slid into her.

The pressure was intense as she forced two fingers into herself. She felt herself open up to the intrusion.

She wrapped her long legs around him and dug her heels into his ass.

"You are really tight. Am I your first?"

"Yes, you're my first now do me."

He pumped in and out of her.

The pressure was building inside of her.

He pumped a few more times and wave after wave started to rush through her. He collapsed on top of her and then rolled off. She rolled over on top of him.

"I'm not paying extra for this."

"I'm going to do you all I want and it's not going to cost you anything. Now shut up and do what I tell you." She lowered herself on him and bounced up and down, liked being in control, giving the orders. She bounced up and down on him.

She finally felt her that wonderful explosion.

He grabbed her ass and pulled her forward and she liked it. She grabbed his chest hairs and used it for leverage and bucked against him.

She exploded again.

"Now do my nipples. Twist them. That's it do them hard."

"You're nipples are so fucking big."

"Do you like them? Do you want to suck on them?

She bent over and let him suck on them as she squirmed all over his shaft.

He let her nipple slip from between his teeth. "You're so tight and hot, you're going to make be come again."

"Not yet," as she let his shaft slip out. She turned around and slipped it back in and really started bucking forwards and backwards. He grabbed her ass and pushed her forward and backwards. Finally she was having one continuous orgasm.

She would ride him for hours until he begged her to stop and then he would sleep. When he woke up he found that she had taken his belt and tied one hand to the bedpost and the other was tied with her garter belt. She was washing his dick and balls.

"Are you in heat lady or totally insane."

"Both. Someone told me that a man can come only once or twice but I wonder how many times they can get hard, let's find out."

She was totally in control and loving. She would be an expert at getting it hard and then she would slam herself down on top of it and tweak her nipple.

She couldn't believe the orgasm continued and continued.

She would buck against him and he would stay hard forever.

"You're so tight your making it sore." She bent down and gave him a gentle kiss.

"I don't care."

She was getting sore down there too but she didn't care she didn't want the orgasm to stop, ever. Over the next several hours she improved her technique for getting him hard and falling in love with being in control. When he finally quit there was a steady throbbing between her legs.

V

As Marilyn stood in the shower she didn't know what was better having that craving finally satisfied or the high from being completely in control. She was running late. Jason was waiting in her office with a look of annoyance. She had thought of him naked, servicing her, and now she was having trouble looking him in the eye. Normally they would have done a mock presentation but now there was no time.

"They are all ready in the conference room."

"Go ahead, I will be right there. I just have to make a quick call."

Jason now looked both annoyed and disappointed."

"Go, go, I will be right there."

She made two quick calls, one to Avalon for Friday night and to Patricia to meet her for supper. She couldn't wait to tell her about the wild weekend.

She took her position at the head of the large conference table. Jason had already passed out the reports. Around the table was the nine member board of Diamond Food Stores waiting for her report on the financial condition of Key Foods that had thirty six stores. As she looked at the group of men that image popped into her mind, she tried to forget it but it consumed her. They were all naked and she was on top of the table sitting in a chair. Her legs were spread and draped over the arms of the chair as she looked each one up and down deciding which one to let service her first. Suddenly she felt nervous like it was her first presentation.

"Excuse me, please, I will be right back."

Marilyn darted down the hallway and into the woman's bathroom. She never had sexual fantasies even when she was young with raging hormones but now they were popping into her mind all the time. Twice that morning, she had mentally undressed men on the train and imagined one taking her in the small space between the two train cars and the other taking her in the lavatory. There was a knock on the door.

"I'll be out in just a minute."

Marilyn quickly wiped her self down and adjusted the cobalt blue business suite. When she opened the bathroom door she expected to see Jason but it was Mr. Clausin a short, dowdy, elderly man with white hair that was very thin on top. He had started the business with a partner.

"Are you alright my dear?"

"I'm fine."

"We haven't been working you too hard?"

"Well, sir, I could use a vacation." Marilyn could not believe how she just blurted it out, had never been that bold before. Normally she just listened and nodded at the appropriate moment with Mr. Clausin.

"Well, how long have been with us, seven years. I worked nine years before I took my first vacation. Since you are a woman I guess we can't expect the same level of dedication."

Marilyn was hurt and a little disappointed. Mr. Clausin had started years ago selling business forms and then expanded to provide business services and when he hired her just out of college they were a fledgling company with offices in the warehouse district.

"I believe my department brought in over a hundred million last year," Marilyn fired back matter-of-factly

"Are you alright, my dear? You take what time you need. We want our best girl working at a hundred percent. Don't we have the Larime merger in two weeks?"

"Yes sir. To be honest, Jason has done most of the prep work and I believe he is ready to do one on his own."

"I hope so, for your sake. I would hate to see you do anything to jeopardize your chance at making partner at the end of the year."

"I will make sure he is ready. Excuse me sir but I have a presentation."

Marilyn strode into the boardroom in control again.

"Sorry, for the delay gentleman. If you turn to page eight of the report,"

Jason shot her a dirty look. She just skipped over the introduction and his part of the presentation. "If you look at the numbers highlighted in blue you can see that Key had gone from paying their prime vendors from every thirty days to once every ninety days increasing their debt load by eighty percent. I have it on good authority that some vendors have refused to make delivery unless they are paid in cash. Normally this increase in debt would force me to recommend that you not make an offer because it would be too much debt to leverage but I believe you can use this to your advantage. A leak to the press about the problems with paying their vendors and their empty shelves will cause a drop in their stock price and therefore you could lower your opening bid by at least thirty percent. You can also use the increase debt to obtain concessions from the unions when their contracts expire in three months. You can then renegotiate with the vendors after the acquisition to get a three to five percent discount by paying within thirty days saving at least ten thousand per store per month. Now let's look at some of the specific numbers."

Marilyn was rubbing her feet when Jason came into her office, glaring. The last three hours had been spent on her feet going over every number and every detail.

"Don't give me that look."

"You cut out my presentation."

"I'll make it up to you."

"How?" They both knew that the presentation was your time to make a good impression which would lead to contacts both personal and professional.

"You're doing the Larime account."

"You're kidding, right?"

"No, it's all yours."

"Where are you going to be?"

"On vacation."

"You are going on vacation? You've never even taken a day off."

"Well it's about time don't you think.

"Do you think I can handle it?"

"You will be when I get done with you."

VI

Patricia's mouth dropped open.

"You look fantastic, you're almost glowing. Did you actually take my advice?"

Over two drinks and dinner Marilyn gave her every detail of her appointment with Avalon and the journey into sexual pleasure.

"Like I told you woman like us have to leave it to the professionals."

"I just have to ask though, how many times have you done it in one day."

"For the longest time my record was twelve but a week ago I did fifteen."

"Oh, my," Marilyn gasped. "I'm going on vacation."

"I hope you are not going to do anything crazy."

"I not sure what I'm going to do."

"Avalon has a vacation island. I was there a couple of years ago. Remember when I told you and everyone else that I was going to Palm Springs. Well, I actually went there. They cater to a wide variety of desires and it's very private, very discrete. You should ask about it at your next appointment."

As they left the restaurant Patricia grabbed her ass.

"Come home with me."

"I can't," Marilyn responded. "I just have too much work to do right now."

Besides right then she was actually satisfied but it would not take long before that hunger between her legs started to grow.

VII

Marilyn not only gave Jason every detail of the process she used, the process developed over years of trail and error and the countless nights spent reading every magazine article she could find but also her inside secrets. The secrets picked up along the way like studying the employee roster trying to find someone who would give her inside information about the company. She showed him how to pose as a customer to find out about their level of service or pose or as a vendor to see what discounts they were giving. He got her contacts at the Internal Revenue Service for copies of corporate tax returns and the returns of the officers to see if they were cooking their books.

On Wednesday, Marilyn gave him several assignments to be checked first thing in the morning. That urge between her legs was growing and she mentally undressed him twice and had to go wipe herself down with a cold washcloth after imaging him servicing her on the top of desk. Now Friday seemed like a year away. She took a cab down to the east side and went into one of those clubs that she had passed by so many times. It was just like she imagined, dark and smelling of booze and cigarettes. After tipping the guy by the door to get her close to the stage, she ordered a gin and tonic. On the stage were two men doing a woman from the front and the back. They were barking obscenities at her but she didn't find it the least bit stimulating and now she was thinking that coming to one of these clubs was a mistake. Marilyn was trying to finish her two drink minimum as quickly as possible and looking for the exit when the curtain closed on the stage and the lights went out. She was now in total darkness. The curtain open and a single spot light lit the stage. On stage was a woman wearing an all black outfit of platform heals, fish net stockings held up by a corset, and push up bra. A black mask hid most of her face. People whooped and hollered as she pranced around the stage cracking a whip. For the first time in her life, Marilyn felt herself get wet. Her heart started to race as a single spotlight started to sweep around the audience as the woman on the stage pointed out the different restraining devices like a magician. The spotlight was now lighting up individuals around the stage for a few seconds and then it would sweep around the room and come to rest on the next man or woman as people cheered their approval or booed their disapproval. Would I actually get up on stage if came to rest on me, she thought. She trembled from excitement and fear. The light bounced from one person to the next faster and faster until finally it came to rest on a man near the stage. She cracked the whip three times to silence the crowd.

With the help of the staff and cheers from the crowd he was led up to the stage. Marilyn noticed that the woman on the stage was short and her legs and arms were a little flabby but she was spellbinding and purely erotic. She showed him off like a magician showing off a magic cabinet. She shackled his writs and ankles and then undid his shirt. She sucked on his nipples until they were hard and then applied nipples clamps to the cheers of the crowd. She ripped off his pants in one motion which common sense told Marilyn that he was part of the act but like the others she didn't care and couldn't wait to see what happened next. She appeared to whip him several times as his manhood bulged in his thong. She pulled his thong down and gulped down his member while giving the crowd a good view of her large, round backside. As she moved away, the crowd, Marilyn included, gasped at his size. She grabbed the bar above his head lifted her self up and then lowed herself on to him. Marilyn, without even thinking about it, slid her hand inside of her panties and started massaging her clit. She quickly looked around but no one was looking at her their eyes were glued to the stage and she wondered how many other people there were doing the same thing. She hoped it was everyone. She exploded as the woman dismounted and another woman brought out a harness that she attached to make his huge, long, member stick straight up. Another woman came out and did a cartwheel and it appeared as if she landed on his upturned shaft. The crowed went crazy, cheering and hollering, and they had there way with him and when the curtain closed Marilyn got up and left feeling her wet panties in the cool night air.

VIII

Marilyn and Jason inspected one of the Buckskin Leather stores. They specialized in western wear and gifts from the southwest. Laramie was getting ready to make a bid for there chain of fifteen stores. Leather wear was a three billion dollar a year industry but never interested Marilyn. She had never experienced the feel of leather against her skin. As Jason went for lunch Marilyn took a cab to the east side. She wanted the same outfit as the woman on the stage but found out that they did not have any for a woman of her stature. Just going and asking, ready to buy, she felt as if some barrier had been crossed. On the one hand her upbringing taught her that it was dirty and good girls didn't wear those kinds of clothes but on the other hand the excitement was intoxicating.

Later, she was at her desk, eating lunch, surfing the internet, finding a world of restraints, whips, leather bondage devices, and a whole array of devices to bring about sexual satisfaction. There were devices for both men and woman all available and could be shipped to home or office. She never new this hidden world existed, a whole industry producing so many devices for sexual satisfaction. She wanted to try everything but showed remarkable restraint and ordered just a few items but the thought of glass wands made her very wet again.

She was trying hard to focus and edit Jason's report but her mind kept wondering, reliving the act on stage wondering what it would be like to do that for a living. She wondered if it was just an obsession that had taken hold of her or did it fulfill some need, some deep seeded need that she never new existed that was below the surface just waiting for the right trigger to bring it to the forefront. She made a few phone calls and learned that the woman that had performed on stage was named Katherine and was working out at a gym on the east side. Marilyn soon found herself at that gym. It took several inquiries until she found her working on the free weights, pumping them with her legs. Upon closer inspection, Marilyn could see that her legs were powerful especially her thighs.

"My name is Marilyn, I caught your performance. It was very good. The company I represent is opening up a club and maybe interested in your services."

"I don't think I'd be interested. I'm happy were I am." She pushed the weights three more times and then stopped and toweled off. "It's all in the legs and the arms. The legs are the most important part. You have to keep them in shape."

"How long have you been doing this?"

"Seven years, I used to do performance art and some exotic dancing but this pays much better. When you have three kids in school and want to put them through college you need more than the few bucks men will stick in your panties."

Marilyn finally noticed the wedding ring on her hand.

"How old are you."

"I'm thirty seven. When I was younger, much younger, I thought about acting and dancing but when you get pregnant at sixteen and have three kids by the time your twenty it defiantly changes things. It's not high art but it's performing and I do four shows a week and I get the day time to be with my kids."

"The company I represent would be willing to pay you forty K a year."

Katherine laughed. "I'm making sixty now, plus tips, so defiantly no thank you."

"Thanks for your time." Her curiosity was satisfied for now. On the way back to the office she made some quick notes on Jason's report. What she really needed was Friday and even more a vacation.

Jason was becoming very annoying. He wanted to go over this figure or that detail. He was a bundle of energy but Marilyn could not find any interest in any of it and it was getting close to her appointment time. She was like that once, dedicated, driven but now couldn't focus or find the desire in it. All I need is a vacation, she thought, and I will come back recharged. She never really had a vacation. Every summer while the kids were out having a good time she was studying. In her junior year she went to business camp and studied for the SAT's. Senior year she spent the summer going over college catalogues narrowing it down between Harvard and Princeton but her father ultimately made the final decision. She bought the books for the first semester, and read them cover to cover. In college the summers were spent doing internships and making contacts. The last year of school she worked full time and still carried a full load of course work. There was no break after graduation, two months of working fulltime at an accounting firm while she went on job interviews, finally deciding on an upstart company where there was more room for advancement. Marilyn finally had to cut Jason off. He had brought in proxy statements for the last five years.

"Read through them, write up a brief summary, and I will look at them first thing in the morning. I have to go."

Leslie was waiting when she entered Avalon's office. She led her into a small conference room. Marilyn noticed she wasn't wearing a business suite but rather a short skirt and tight blouse. She was a small woman at five two and Marilyn towered over her. She had a large chest for a small woman. It had been hidden under her business suite but now it was in plain view and Marilyn liked the looks of it and then, for the first time, she wondered if she was turning into a lesbian.

"I just wanted to see if you were satisfied with our service?"

"I'm very satisfied."

"You don't have any questions or problems with our fees."

Marilyn thought their fees were obscenely high but didn't care.

"Everything is fine."

This delay was now causing her more anguish than Jason was inflecting earlier.

"Here is my business card. On the back is my home number, if you need or want anything feel free to call me at home."

"Patricia told me that you have vacation packages."

"Yes, we have our own private island. It's very exclusive. I will have a packet of information for you at the receptionist desk. You can pick it up when you leave."

Leslie escorted her to the therapy room. Once the door closed Marilyn stripped in mere moments, got in the chair, and positioned it so she was sitting up and her bottom was at the edge. She wanted to be ready, wanted to feel orgasm after orgasm. It was like a drug now. She was a bit surprised when Kim came in and not Leslie.

"How are we doing today?"

"Fine."

"What can I do for you today?" she asked and then massaged Marilyn's inner thigh.

"I want you to do me and do me hard."

"Are you sure you wouldn't want a man? We have several that could service you,"

Kim asked as she massaged her clit and then slipped her middle finger inside of her. The thought of being a lesbian popped into her mind again. It was true she had checking out woman more, more in a sexual way but she had also been checking out men. She fantasized about men when she did herself. She finally decided that she wasn't a lesbian. It just didn't matter who was doing her as long she got what she craved.

"No, it doesn't matter. Just do me." She was a little embarrassed because she almost begging.

"You are much more open than your last visit." Kim unbuttoned her nurse's uniform and let it fall to the floor. She was wearing nothing but a lacy bra and thong. Marilyn had been right: she was really built with large, firm, breasts, and a round firm bottom that stuck out. She went to a cabinet and pulled out a pair of latex panties, slipped them over her thong, and then attached a long, thin dildo to it.

"Please, take off your bra; I want to see your chest." What she really wanted to cry out was take off your bra I want to see those enormous tits, but couldn't bring herself to say it.

Kim took off the bra and her large, full breasts hung free.

"You have such a nice chest. I wish mine were like that."

"You don't need them. You are very attractive, and have a nice, athletic body." Marilyn thought she was just being nice. She was any thing but attractive and built like her father, tall, and lean.

"Has anyone every done your ass before? I could make love to it if you want me too?" Paula asked as she worked the tip of the dildo in and out of her. Marilyn was intrigued but was all out of patience so she said, "Quit fooling around and do me."

Then Marilyn realized that she was teasing her letting the anticipation build, making her want it more than anything and it was really driving her crazy.

"I don't want to hurt you."

"I don't care, ram it in and do me." Marilyn grabbed her tits and pulled her forward. Paula grabbed the back of her neck lunged forward taking Marilyn's breathe away.

She worked the dildo in and out using her ample hips. Marilyn liked the felling of it plunging into her. She pulled Paula closer driving in her tongue. She tongued her for several minutes then bit her lower lip.

"Now do me you little bitch."

She felt in control and loved it. Marilyn put her head on the back of the chair and closed her eyes as wave after wave went through her body. Her thighs were getting wet and she loved that feeling too.

"Have you got anything bigger; I want to be ripped open?"

"Are you sure? I don't want to hurt you," Paula responded as she changed the angle of her movements bucking up hard lifting her ass off the chair.

"Yes, I want something bigger. I expect to be serviced."

Paula withdrew the dildo and Marilyn felt a rush of fluid escape her. Paula brought out another dildo from the cabinet, a few inches longer, and much bigger around. She lined it up and with one motion had all of it inside her. Marilyn gasped at its presence. It filled her so completely. Her insides were molding around it, expanding to accommodate it as orgasm after orgasm raced through her. Paula started to pull it out.

"No, leave it in, all the way in."

Marilyn lowered the back of the chair so she was laying flat.

"Now lay on top of me."

Marilyn grabbed her small ass and rocked her back and forth on top of her. The dildo barely moved inside of her but it was enough as the most wonderful feeling ever went through her. Marilyn tried to keep track of the orgasms but it was impossible. It was one continuous orgasm. Paula sucked on her nipple, gently at first; pushing it around with her tongue then more forcefully until her teeth were grading it and at the same time she worked the other one between her fingers.

"You have such large, delicious nipples. Would you like me to do your ass now?" Marilyn was content to lie like this forever but she wanted to try everything.

"Yes."

"Would you like to keep the dildo inside of you?"

"Please."

Paula unhooked the dildo and got off and Marilyn rolled over onto her stomach. Paula lowered the bottom part of the chair so she hung slightly over the edge. Paula kissed one check as she massaged the other. She stuck her tongue between her cheeks and Marilyn jumped.

"You don't find it pleasing?"

"Yes, I've never felt anything like that back there."

Paula sucked and kissed from the top to the bottom. Marilyn was grasping each side of the chair for dear life. She sucked on the tender flesh at the bottom and Marilyn moaned her approval. She kissed, sucked, and bit her way up and down between her cheeks. Marilyn never felt anything so deliciously wicked. She looked back; wanting to see what she was doing and couldn't believe that her whole face was buried between her cheeks. Suddenly her tongue found her most private area and she lay frozen not moving a muscle. She never knew that spot was so sensitive. Marilyn reached back and spread her cheeks wanting her to have better access. Her insides gripped the dildo and wave after wave went through her. Paula got up went to the cabinet and brought over a very thin, vibrator. Marilyn gave it her approval by sucking on it and getting it very, wet. Paula gently inserted it while sucking on that sensitive area at the bottom of her checks. Marilyn was being invaded and she liked it. She never thought of that spot in a sexual way but now her mind was racing with the possibilities. What other things could she use to invade her body, would they all feel different, and would they all give her pleasure like this? Paula turned the vibrator to maximum and Marilyn gripped the sides of the chair again as the vibrations traveled through her from the top of her head to the tip of her toes. Marilyn buried her face in the chair as the two vibrators felt like they were meeting somewhere inside. She experienced the most intense orgasm. Paula worked both vibrators, in and out, in a nice steady rhythm and the only thing Marilyn could do was grunt and moan.

"Do you want me to stop?"

"Never, I could take it forever. You've awakened an insatiable monster."

IX

Marilyn looked through the material the receptionist had given her. At first glance it looked like your standard island resort, a hotel with plenty of beach front with all the immentites, tennis courts, horseback riding, scuba diving, and saunas. But the twist was on the last page, in the last paragraph, where it said that private villas were available upon request and that the entire staff was dedicated to fulfill their sexual fantasies. Leslie had handwritten-call me with any questions- and her phone number.

Marilyn picked up the phone but put it back down. She paced around the apartment wondering if this is what she really wanted to do. There was no doubt that she needed a vacation. Now that the, insatiable monster, as she now referred to it, had been awakened it need attention. She thought if it got enough attention then it would be satisfied and she could go back to the way it was before. She picked up phone and called the toll free number and operator told her there would be non-stop flight to Houston and then a charter flight with one stop in Mexico City. Marilyn did not ask about the cost and they never offered any information knowing it would be very expensive but she didn't care. I deserve it, she thought. The flight was leaving early Saturday morning and would return following Thursday; good she thought it would give me the weekend to get ready for work. After hanging up, she realized that there were still a lot of questions. What to bring? What not to bring? She picked up the brochure and looked through it again but there was no information. Finally she decided to call Leslie and just leave a message. She was surprised it was her cell phone number.

"Leslie, its Marilyn."

"It's nice to hear from you. How can I help you?" Marilyn noticed her voice had a much less business tone.

"I made a reservation at the resort."

"Good for you, I'm sure you will have a wonderful time."

"I was hoping there was list of things that I should take."

"There should have been one attached to the brochure."

"I'm sorry," Marilyn responded, "I looked through everything and I didn't see it."

"I will be more than happy to run it over to you."

"That's not necessary you can just send it to the office. I don't want to interrupt your weekend."

"Nonsense, it will be my pleasure. Besides if you're like me you want to spend the weekend getting ready. I will bring it over at seven."

"That will be fine, thank you."

It was true Marilyn wanted to spend the weekend getting ready. She wanted to lay everything out on the bed so everything could be accounted for, every contingency covered, the way her father, a career military man, had taught her. If she had any plans of going swimming she would need a new swim suite. The one she had was when she was on the varsity swim team in college. She did like to swim but it also brought back unpleasant memories of summer camp. She was always the best swimmer but the girls and boys made fun of her large, bony, frame. Surely, I am past that sort of thing, she thought.

After two hours of trying on bikinis at the mall, she had given up. They all reviled way too much of her pale, skin. The clerk finally suggested a swim dress and she tried it on. Even the smallest one hung on her like an oversized tent. It was a suite for some one older but given the alternatives she decided to take it. She also took a Sheath suit even though her small breasts didn't fill out the preformed cups it did show off her lovely bottom and shapely legs. She would wait until Leslie brought over the list to pick out anything else.

On subway ride home she decided that it was going to be the best vacation of her life. Vacations with her mother and father were always grueling affairs. Her father's slightest suggestion always seemed like commands. She always wondered what her mother did those summers when she was away at camp and he was out to sea. Maybe it was the only time she could do what she really wanted to do and that was what Marilyn was going to do on this vacation.

The doorbell rang promptly at seven. When Marilyn opened the door she was surprised that Leslie was not dressed in a business suite even though it was Saturday. Instead she was wearing a tight pair of slacks and even a tighter pull over top. A large carry all bag hung from one shoulder. Leslie came in and sat down on the couch and took the list out of her bag and handed it to Marilyn.

"I hope that gives you all the information you wanted. It is very hot down there this time of year. For Some one with your skin tone, I would suggest at least a thirty sun block. It's very sunny and I would hate to see your vacation ruined by nasty sunburn."

Marilyn only glanced at the list and then pretended to look at it. What she was really looking at was Leslie's ample breasts and the two little round circles protruding from the tight material of her top.

"If you decide to go scuba diving or take advantage of the charter fishing everything will be provided. Basically you just have to take your clothes and your personal care items. Would you like some suggestions on what clothes to bring?"

"Yes," Marilyn said sitting down on the couch. She sat very close to Leslie. Leslie moved even closer. Marilyn couldn't take her eyes off those two circles protruding from her chest. She knew they weren't her nipples they were to perfectly round and there was another indentation running down the front of her top to her waist.

"It is normally eighty five or ninety during the day. At night it cools off very nicely and if the wind is off the ocean it can feel quite cool so I suggest shorts or lose skirts for the day time and a dress or slacks in the evening and a light jacket, just cool, comfortable clothes. There are one or two get-togethers at night, just to meet some of the other guests but only if you want to, for that I would suggest an evening dress. For you I would suggest a dark dress, very short to show off your lovely legs with a deep neck line and backless."

She tried to hide her bony knees under the coffee table.

"Have you been there recently," Marilyn asked.

"Yes, two years ago," Leslie replied as she slipped her hand between her back and the couch grazing her skin. "I was lucky enough to meet another gust there that I was completely combatable with. We had a lovely week together."

Marilyn's mind started to race. She wanted this little woman; she wanted her between her legs, to command her, to control her but didn't know how Leslie felt. She was getting every accustomed to having sex with a woman finding it both comfortable and satisfying but with Leslie it had been strictly professional. Was this professional, was she just interested in providing another service for a fee or was it more. Marilyn could not believe that she would actually want her. It had to be her way of subscribing more business.

Leslie touched her knee and Marilyn jumped, banging the coffee table. Leslie pressed on moving her hand up her legs and quickly massaging the sensitive flesh of her upper thigh.

"You do have lovely legs."

"Are you on the clock," Marilyn asked bluntly.

"I'm on my own time."

"Am I going to have to pay for this?"

"If you do what I want maybe I will pay you."

Then Leslie slid up her top ever, so slowly and Marilyn saw the most erotic thing ever. In her nipples were to large, gold, rings and running down from the rings were gold chains that ran down and into her slacks.

"Yes, they run all the way to my clit."

"Doesn't that hurt?"

"Slightly, I like it when it hurts."

Leslie grabbed the back of her neck and pulled her close and used her tongue and lips like fine tools, tools of seduction. Marilyn pulled on the chains and could feel her orgasm vibrating though the strands of metal and was happy that she could satisfy her so quickly but jealous that her own needs had not been met.

"I want you to dominate me. I want you to hurt me," Leslie said almost pleading as she pulled out latex panties with an attached dildo and a riding crop from the bag.

Marilyn really wanted to abuse this little woman but she also wanted her own needs met so for the first time in her life she took control. She stood up and looked down at her.

"I will take you but first you will please me."

"You promise to take me and abuse me," Leslie replied as her trembling hands unbuttoned Marilyn's shorts.

"Only if you please me first."

"I've wanted you ever since the first time we met."

"Then prove it to me."

Marilyn never felt so aroused and the feeling of being in complete control was a new kind of high she never felt before. Leslie got on the large, glass, coffee table and Marilyn straddled her, lowering herself as Leslie reached out with her tongue but Marilyn stayed just out of reach.

"Please let me have it. I want to please you."

"Do you think that you can?"

"Yes, please, please, I know I can, let me please you."

Marilyn lowered herself and in moments her lips and tongue were all over her. She never felt anything so delicious. With Paula it was so clinical but with Leslie it was pure passion. Marilyn felt so alive, so sensual, so in control as orgasm after orgasm went through her. She let her drink her juice and then she cleaned up her thighs with her tongue. She got off and stood beside her.

"Have I pleased you mistress?" Leslie asked.

"Not yet," Marilyn said as she turned around and placed her ass right above her face.

"I suppose you find this disgusting."

"No mistress, I will service any part of your body." Marilyn just loved the way she fell into the role of being submissive, of being her sexual servant.

"Do me good and you may just get a good beating and screwing. Not that you really deserve it."

Marilyn almost lost control as she tongued the most sensitive parts and inserted her tongue inside of her most private part. Marilyn finally had to submit when she sprayed juice all over the coffee table.

Marilyn put on the latex panties with attached dildo and Leslie quickly got on her hands and knees. Marilyn stood behind her and she slid back desperately trying to find the dildo.

"Please, mistress, I would be so grateful if you would take me."

She very slowly and gently pushed in the dildo as she bent over and gently moved her rings though her nipples and clit.

"I would be so grateful mistress, if you would hurt me inside."

Marilyn plowed the dildo in and out with all the force she could muster and with every thrust Leslie thanked her and praised her and Marilyn loved the control she had over this little woman. She learned quickly how to control her orgasms, bringing her to the brink and then stopping until she was begging for her to continue, begging for that release she so desperately craved. Marilyn did her until her hips started to ache and then collapsed totally spent. Leslie slept on the couch and twice during the night she summoned her to the bedroom to service her, to satisfy her needs like a servant.

On Sunday they went shopping together and Leslie helped pick out new outfits for the vacation and Marilyn was pleased when they got home and Leslie got down on her knees and begged to stay another night. So Marilyn made her strip and then made her fix her dinner, bath her, do her hair, and massage her. She would pull on the chains if she did the slightest thing that displeased her. Leslie serviced her in the kitchen, the bathroom and several times in the bedroom and after sufficient begging and pleading Marilyn found new ways to abuse her with the dildo and riding crop.

When Marilyn awoke she found a note from Leslie saying that her nipples and clit hurt and thanking her for the lovely abusive weekend and that the thinking of them together would satisfy her in the lonely nights ahead. Marilyn was sad that it had to end.

X

    As the train got closer to the city, I've become addicted to sex, she thought. Once she got a taste of carnal knowledge it was like a drug, she craved it but could she control it. As the train slowed and made its way into the station, Marilyn decided to take back her life that more than likely she would never hear from Leslie again except in a purely professional manner and, like Patricia, use Avalon once every few months or even better only when it was absolutely necessary. She would cancel the vacation but she had no idea what their cancellation policy was and how much it would cost her. She would just stay home. There was no way to pull Jason off the current project with out him throwing a major fit and she suspected that he was running to Mr. Clausin at every opportunity trying to sabotage her career. She would work on the next project from home, go to the office late a night when everyone was gone and know one had to know. As she walked through the station she looked at the large clock hanging from the ceiling and it was just after 9:00 am and realized that she was going to be late again but even that was a foreign concept because she never had regular working hours. There was no home life. How did other people work nine to five and go home and have sex with their partners and then get up and do it again. She would stay in her office for days, working until she was exhausted; she had never worked a regular schedule. It only felt late because normally she would be in the office at seven, eight at the very latest. She called Avalon and the receptionist was going to put her through to Leslie but she didn't want to talk to her; didn't know what to say having no experience with dealing professionally with someone she had slept with but it was more than that she virtually no experience in dealing with anyone who she had sexual experience with and they hadn't just merely slept together they had wild, kinky sex that boarded on the bizarre the kind of sex she couldn't tell anyone about because it was what most people would consider perverted but just the thought of Leslie excited her and part of her wanted to make an appointment right away because as she was getting dressed earlier she had thought of more bizarre and kinky things to do like rubbing herself up and down on those chains and soaking them with her orgasm. I have to stop thinking about those kinds of things, she thought, and then asked the receptionist about their cancellation policy and found out it was thirty days. She told her that she was just checking and that she had every intention of going. Just as she was about to walk out to where all cabs were lined up two hookers came into the station. Marilyn stopped and stared at them. I wish that I could be hooker, she thought. She could not believe she actually thought of that and even if she had the body for it, which she knew she didn't, would I actually do something like that. Marilyn sat down on the nearest bench and watched them walk to the restrooms. The way they exposed themselves with short shirts and tight blouses that barely contained their breasts always fascinated her but now it had gone from mere fascination to desire. She sat on the bench watching their cheeks work in the tight skirts and actually wanting to be a hooker. They were always in control, deciding who they were going to have sex with and for how much. Just the thought of getting paid to have sex made her get excited but she wasn't sure why it excited her so. Was it because she now had her first real taste of sex and had developed an insatiable appetite for it or was it the part of being in control. Was it because her father had always controlled her? He had scared away the only two boys that showed any interest in her, picked out her college, and her major, and even now, from the grave, he was controlling her still, working a job to please him.

When Marilyn walked into her office, Jason was at her desk.

"What's up with you anyway? You're the one that scheduled the meeting for ten."

Marilyn looked at her watch. "I still have twelve minutes." Actually she had forgotten all about the meeting and at that moment was thinking that she wanted to make Jason get down underneath the desk and service her as she dug her heels into him. I have to really stop thinking about things like that, but on the other hand, she thought, it was becoming a nice diversion.

"Your mother has called for the third time and she is holding on line three."

Marilyn walked over to her desk and quickly transferred the call to her cell phone.

"Go ahead to the conference room, I will be there in minute," Marilyn said as she headed for her bathroom.

"Hello, mother."

"I called you several times this weekend. Where have you been?"

"I've been busy mother."

"You know Pricilla McGovern; I play tennis with her at the country club?"

"Yes, I know her. I have a meeting in a couple of minute's mother."

"Well, we were playing on Saturday and she said that her husband had told her that he had heard that you had been taken off an assignment and reprimanded."

Marilyn had learned very early in her career the power of the gossip mill. David McGovern was one of the senior partners and had given Marilyn's father regular updates on her performance.

"No mother, I've never been reprimanded and I'm just letting one of my assistants take over while I'm on vacation."

Marilyn cringed. She didn't want her mother to know anything about her vacation until the last possible moment.

"Vacation, you never mentioned a vacation before. Are you going to house in the Hamptons?

"No mother, I'm going to a resort in Mexico."

That sealed it for Marilyn. She was back to original plan. Go on vacation, get it out of her system, and come back and rededicate herself to her career.

"I hope you are alright. I know how woman your age can go through a midlife crises especially with no husband and no children."

Marilyn sat down on the toilet and sighed.

"I'm fine mother. I just need a break. I deserve a break. I have to go there is meeting right now."

"Please call me; we must have lunch at the club. I just want make sure you are alright."

Marilyn walked into the conference room and took note of Jason rolling his eyes.

"So, are your reports ready?" No one answered. Marilyn flipped though her day planner.

"The formal presentation will be on Wednesday."

"It's scheduled for Friday," Jason responded sharply. "We are not meeting with the clients until next week."

"You have to be ready for anything, able to think on your feet. Like I told you before, you do your research, come to your recommendation, and then build your supporting documentation. That is what the client is paying for. Your supporting documentation is just for their accounts to look at afterwards. You have to be able to make a recommendation as quickly as possible in the process. Remember the Toshita account? That was moved up two weeks. The presentation will be on Wednesday."

They all groaned. That will teach him, Marilyn thought as she sat down, crossed her legs, and folded her arms. She was in control but it didn't have that excitement of sexual control.

"Begin." Marilyn said.

"Horton Hancock has been over stating their profits for the last three quarters," Jason said. "There plants in Kentucky and Alabama have been operating at only thirty percent capacity and there have not been any capital improvements in the last decade."

Marilyn let him drone on as she mentally undressed him. She had never thought about any of her staff in a sexual way before they were just workers, report producers. She knew nothing about their personal lives figured Jason was gay or dominated by an overbearing mother, figured that he could service her very nicely with the proper training. Andrea was next. She almost didn't hire her mainly because of the way she dressed at the interview wearing a very, short, skirt and a see through blouse that showed off her nice chest. She didn't have a college degree but had decent grades from a well know business school. Of course, it didn't hurt that her father was a congressman.

Marilyn was going to talk to her about wearing more professional outfits but figured that Andrea would just think that she was jealous because she did not have the body for it. Marilyn could not help but notice how some of the male clients would pay special attention to her and now she thought it probable help business. She wondered if she was very sexually active or did she just go home and please herself knowing that the men were drooling over her.

Bill was last. He was tall and athletic. She figured he worked out a couple times a week and imagined that he was well hung. She wondered what it would be like to be serviced by someone so well hung and so athletic. Would she have powerful orgasms even more powerful that the ones she had with Leslie?

Marilyn was snapped out of her wonderful daydream when she finally noticed that no one was talking.

"Everything looks good. The final presentation is on Wednesday at one."

Marilyn took a good look at Andrea's cleavage as she bent over the table to gather up her papers and wondered what it would be like to kiss that beautiful thing.

"And where will you be?" Jason asked. Marilyn quickly thought of a whip and a collar around his neck as he spent hours between her legs.

"Well, you are in charge. For the next two days, I will be your assistant."

And she was. For two days she did everything he asked without question, even went out and got food and coffee. Twice Jason pointed out mistakes that she had made the kind of mistakes that she used to catch. She was trying very hard to push all those thoughts from her mind, trying very hard not to think of anything but work, trying not to have any sexual thoughts of Leslie, Jason or Patricia or anyone else. She scolled herself after having a quick orgasm in her private bathroom while thinking about Patricia and how she had satisfied her twice without anything in return and how next time it would be different, how she would dominate her, whip her, and make her completely satisfy her before she even thought about her own needs. After that episode, she was back concentrating on work and vowing that after the vacation she would cast out all those wicked thoughts and actions and get back to normal.

XI

Marilyn was glad to be back in charge after the practice formal presentation. She made three pages of notes during the presentation. There were major holes all over the place but blamed herself for not having her mind where it should have been earlier in the process. Maybe I'm just being overly critical, she thought. So she circled three items on her note pad that were must fixes.

"Very good, but there are a couple of things, first, how can you say that you will get concessions out of the union when their contract expires if don't talk to the head of the union. Andrea, the union office is right here in town so go down there and see what you can find out." What she really wanted to say was go shake your sweet body down at the union hall and I'm sure they will tell you anything you want to know.

"The plants in Kentucky and Alabama have been stone walling us for two weeks on faxing us their production reports and expenses accounts. Bill, in my G drive is a court order I scanned from another project so just change the names and dates and fax it and tell them the sheriff will be serving the original in forty eight hours if they don't comply."

"We can't really do that, can we?" asked Bill.

"No, but they don't know that."

"Jason, I totally agree with your recommendation that their selling price is way too high. So, Alcon will ask what a fair price would be. Of course that will be another project and fee for the company but if we do it know we will be way ahead of the game. So you and I will need to cost out their entire operation right down to cost of the chairs and tables in the cafeteria. Most of the information we already have so we just need to put it in a formal presentation. Good job everyone but we still have a lot of work to do. The last presentation is Friday at three so get to it."

XII

At the airport, Marilyn felt naked, stripped, no lab top, no day planner, no cell phone. She had skillfully dodged all of her mother's phone calls and had called and left a message right before she had left the cell phone on the kitchen table.

She was running late. The mock presentation had run late but thought it was very good; they were ready, but it gave her just enough time to run home, throw everything into one rollaway and shoulder bag and catch a cab to the airport.

People were filing down the gangway. She spotted Leslie talking to a couple over by the windows. It made Marilyn wonder how many people on board the flight were with Avalon. Leslie finally came over and handed her an envelope.

"Have a safe flight and a wonderful vacation. There will be an Avalon representative in Houston to direct you to the charter flight," she said, very professional, with out making eye contact. Marilyn was both relieved but a bit disappointed. On the back of the envelope Leslie had written please see me when you get back. Inside the envelope were various coupons for free items or buy one get one free from various merchants. Marilyn shoved into her shoulder bag. I will throw the envelope away later, she thought. She would have no need for what they shared when the vacation was over.

When the seat belt sign went off, Marilyn reclined the seat as far as possible. She was exhausted, had barely slept the last two nights. There were only little cat naps on her office couch. She had spent the last two days compling figures and preparing reports. She had to admit that it was draining. In the beginning it was exciting, trying to beat the clock, racing against the deadline, but the excitement was gone, it was just draining. I just need a little vacation, she thought as she drifted off to sleep.

The flight attendant shook her ever so gently but Marilyn was startled.

"Please, fasten your seat belt we will be arriving shortly."

Marilyn looked out the window and in a few moments saw the terminal and runway lights coming up fast. She had slept through the whole flight. I must have really been tired, she thought. She looked around the plane and then it dawned on her that she was on vacation, really on vacation. What will I do? She thought. There were no reports to look over; no phone calls to make, no figures to balance; a whole week were nothing was planned. How could that be? As the planes tires hit the runway she was reaching into her shoulder bag and for the Avalon brochure, she had to at least mentally plan the next couple of days, the ultimate planner still at work.

She checked in with the Avalon representative and was informed it would be about forty five minutes until her bags were transferred and the charter flight was ready. She needed coffee. At the coffee shop she started to form a plan. First breakfast, then each day a new activity, one day scuba diving, one day horse back riding, one day maybe tennis, and at night, what would she do at night, she was accustomed to being at the office at night working until she passed out on her couch with the lab top still on and in her lap. It was puzzling. She had no idea what to do at night.

"Excuse me, but you look familiar."

One of the oldest pick up lines in the world, Marilyn thought, as she looked up and saw a man about her father's age. She brushed her slight bangs out of her face.

"Don't you work on the street?"

"Clausin, Nash, and Finch."

"Oh yes, the merger barons, now I remember, you handled our merger with Keystone Securities about a year ago. I'm with National Insurance."

Marilyn remembered now. They were one of the biggest corporate retirement planners in the country.

"Are you in here on business?"

"Actually I'm on my way to Mexico for a vacation."

"Good for you, you look like you need it."

Marilyn had to laugh. Did I really look as bad as I feel, she thought.

"So what do you have planned in Mexico."

"I don't know yet."

"Well, sometimes the best vacations are the ones where you don't plan anything. Well I have to go; I don't want to miss my flight. I hope you have a good time."

"Thank you."

That was it Marilyn thought, no schedules, no plans, just do what you feel like doing when you want to do it. She didn't have to be like her father where every minute was planned.

There were about twenty people standing in the gateway as the plane was now ready for boarding. She recognized the older couple that Leslie had been talking to in the terminal. There were several couples with rest of the people appeared to be unattached, some men, more women then men, of varying age groups, several that Marilyn figured were about her age.

Marilyn could not believe that when she got on the plane she was taken to her own private compartment. It was a jumbo 757 but they had taken out all the seats and made little compartments. She had her own bar, small bathroom, couch, desk and large chair. There was a television built into the wall. The attendant pointed out the phone. "We will be leaving shortly we are waiting for one more passenger. Once we are airborne if you need anything just pick up the phone. We have a full kitchen in the back, and the menu is by the phone." The menu included, lobster, steak, salmon, salads, she was getting famished but there were so many choices. She sat down the couch, thankful to be able to finally stretch out.

There was a knock on the door.

"Yes."

An attendant came in. "Miss Conners."

"Yes."

"Here is your bag just in case you needed anything."

Behind him a woman walked buy wearing a large hat and sunglasses and Marilyn thought she had seen her somewhere before but wasn't sure where. Defiantly not from work but she had seen her before, perhaps on television.

"When we reach the island the bag will be transferred to your villa."

"Thank you."

Marilyn stretched out on the couch, laying her head on the soft pillows, wondering who the woman was and thinking that she may like this vacation after all. All of her muscles started to relax, started to unwind, and she couldn't believe that their was no work to do, not now, not tomorrow, or even the next day, at that moment a week seemed like a life time.

Then she quickly sat up as it hit her, the small frame, the two moles on the side of her neck, even with the large hat and sunglasses, it had to be her. It had to be Abigail, Abby from the daytime drama Desires. Marilyn's only vice. She got hooked in college and would tape all the shows and watch them on the weekend; sometimes it would be two weeks until she could catch up on all the plot twists. She would make popcorn, get in her pajamas and watch show after show. Abby was her favorite, always in control, doing anything to get what she wanted. She was so attractive and elegant. On the show, she was the vixen, so charming and likeable but behind their backs, scheming to thwart any chance they had at happiness and sleeping with anyone who would help her climb up the corporate latter or do her bidding but cross her and she would cut you off at the knees or get her way by pitting one character against the other.

Marilyn tried hard to remember her real name, not her stage name, it was McKenzie Taylor, she thought. While she ate she tried to write a note wanted to meet her not just to get an autograph but to find out what she was really like and once they got to the resort she would have to respect her privacy so this was her one and only chance. She wrote several and threw them away not wanting to sound just like some obsessed fan. Finally she just wrote, I hate to invade your privacy but I would so much like to meet you, we share something in common. The attendant at first refused to deliver the note until she offered a fifty dollar tip. After two hours she had convinced herself that the attendant never delivered the note or the last thing she would want to do is meet some half crazed fan until there a light rap on her cabin door and there she stood.

"Please, please come in."

She was so small and piete, only five two, and very thin, much thinner than she appeared on television.

"I guess my disguise didn't work. What gave me away?

"Your moles I sure no one else would have noticed. I have been watching you since college and I would know those moles anywhere."

"I was going to have them removed early in my career," she replied, as she touched her neck, touching the two tiny black dots that were so promident against her pale skin. "But they are sort of my trademark now. Funny, I used to cover them with pearls or a scarf. They are just two tiny little dots. It's funny how we can become obsessed about things"

She sat down on the couch. "You are very tall, and attractive. Are you in show business? You said we had something in common."

"Yes, we are both workaholichs. I read somewhere that it was written into your contract that you had to be in almost every scene."

"It's true. It's not because I'm a control freak like the tabloids report, it's just that I just can't stand sitting around. If you are not in almost every scene you can sit around in your trailer for hours. That would drive me crazy. There is so much waiting around. I swear the unions are going to be death of this industry. You can't move a cable six inches without two union guys and a foreman. It takes a week of twelve to fourteen hour days just to get one episode shot. And what business are you in?

"I work on Wall Street. I work for a company that evaluates mergers and acquisitions. This is my first vacation in seven years." Marilyn was afraid she was babbling.

"Oh, dear, I know just how you feel. When I first started, you would have to drag me off the set kicking and screaming. I had to be there every moment. When we weren't shooting Desires I was trying to get parts in other shows. I was involved with six charities. I am starting to slow down, to relax more. I guess it's about time since I'm nearing sixty."

Marilyn shook her head couldn't believe that she was that old.

"You don't look half that age."

"Now you are just trying to flatter me. I wish that I could say it's from healthy living but it's not. I really don't do anything special and I'm a terrible junk food junkie. It's all in the genes. I was a late bloomer. I still had braces and a face full of acne when I entered college. I was going to be a veterinarian. I'm just a farm girl from Nebraska. But then the braces came off and my skin cleared up. I was asked to be in a production of Street Car and I was hooked. I never wanted to do anything else after that. Do you like what you are doing?"

"I don't know. I did at first but now I don't know."

"You are very fortunate if you are passionate about your work and can make a living at it."

Marilyn couldn't believe she was sitting there talking to her like she was just a regular person. She wanted to find out why she was going to the resort. Was it to have some sexual deviant behavior satisfied the kind of behavior that if people would find about would end her career? She was torn because she was so curious but still knowing full well it was none of her business.

"So you have watched the show a long time."

"I started watching in the seventies."

"Wow, now that does make me feel old."

"I like your character. She is so assertive. She doesn't take anything from anyone. I like the way she stands up to the other men when it comes to business."

"Yes, not every one can get paid to be a stone, cold, bitch."

They both laughed.

"She is defiantly not a role model. She is a back stabbing, power hungry bitch but I hope in some small way it helped woman become more assertive especially in the work place. That is why I got involved in the plight of battered woman."

Marilyn was getting nervous wanted so desperately to know why she was going to the resort and felt like time was running out.

"Is this your first time to the resort?"

"Yes," Marilyn replied.

"Did you come to have your sexual fantasies fulfilled?"

"Yes"

"And what are they?"

"I don't know for sure." Marilyn thought she sounded coy or evasive but it was true. She did not want to tell her that she thought that she was addicted to sex and this was chance at purification.

"Then you should try everything, anything. Believe me it's a once in a lifetime opportunity to explore, to enjoy yourself."

"And what is yours? I'm sorry; I shouldn't have asked it's really none of my business."

"It's perfectly alright. It's really not very exocitic. I liked to be romanced. I like to be brought flowers, to have candlelit dinners, to walk along the beach and hold hands. A normal relationship is impossible for me. I go out with a man more than once and tabloids are full of stories and most men don't want to mess with that. So I come here to have dates and be romanced like a normal person. Last time there was a sweet man named Gerald. He was very romantic, very kind and sweet. Of course it didn't hurt that the stud muffin was only twenty five."

They both giggled like schoolgirls. McKenzie curled up her legs on the couch and they talked like old college roommates. When she left Marilyn had changed her mind again. She would purge her sexual addition not by abstaining but by trying anything that caught her fancy and after she had sampled different things then she would be free, her sexual appetite would be quenched. She had forgotten to get her autograph but it was just as well she thought, she could never tell anyone where or how she got it.

Jeeps were waiting when the plane touched down. Their bags were quickly transferred and they were quickly driven to their villas. She was taken to one of the smallest villas. It was one large room with a small kitchen and a dinning area with a view of the ocean, a large king sized bed, amour, and dresser. The villas were separated by a wooded area. A fence went around the large deck for complete privacy. On the deck were a hot tub, barbeque grill, lounge chairs, and a table with an umbrella. Marilyn was just starting to breath in the freshest air in years when there was a knock on the door. A tall young man with blond hair and a perfect tan was holding a basket of fruit and muffins.

"Good evening my name is Gerald."

She checked his picture identification that hung on his shirt and then let him in.

"I will be your personal attendant while you are staying here. Here is my card you can call me twenty four hours a day."

"Twenty four hours! When do you sleep?"

"I don't."

"I know that feeling."

"If there is nothing you require I will let you get settled in."

Marilyn stepped out on the deck. A wooden sidewalk led down to the ocean lit my small lanterns. The moon was full and reflecting off the ocean. It was beautiful. Marilyn wondered what time it was and what day it was but then decided she didn't care. She was exhausted. In the bathroom was a soaking tub and she never seen so many different soaps and bath oils. She poured passion fruit into the tub and slid in. Her body responded as she felt her muscles relax and her mind responded, for the fist time in a long time, by shutting down. Her mind went blank. She didn't think about work. Her mind and body was totally relaxed, at peace.

She made only one mental note as she crawled in between the sheets. The only order of business for tomorrow was to have fun.

XIII

When she woke up it was still dark. When she awoke again, there was a dream about her father. He still haunted her from the grave. There was more daylight coming in from the windows. She made coffee, triple strength, wondering how she was going to make it through the day without the two or three triple expressos that got her through the day. Massive doses of caffeine had become the drug of choice for just about everyone she knew. She opened up the sliding doors to the deck and it was just as beautiful in the daylight as the sun glistened off the ocean. She sat down in the lounge chair and sipped the coffee. The only noise was the lapping of the ocean on the beach and a few birds in far off trees. The din of the city was gone for it was never silent not even in the dead of night. She was sitting in the chair with just a pair of panties, no bra, nothing else. She wasn't completely sure no one could see her so she got up and found a bathrobe, started looking through the brochure as she ate muffins and fruit and tried to get her caffeine fix. It was well done with full color photographs. There was a small city seven miles away with souvenir shops, bars, night clubs in addition to the three restaurants and two bars at the resort. On the last two pages was a list of sexual activities:

Massage
Sexual Massage
Consenual Rape
Gang Bang
Intimate Encounters
Male Escorts
Female Escorts
One on one Male
One on one Female
Group sex

Erotic dancers
Lap dancers
Female domination
Male domination
Interracial encounters.
Sex therapy
Sexual devices
Erotic films
Erotic printed material.

At the very end, in small print, it said minors and animals will not be provided at any price and to call for current celebrity encounters.

Marilyn had to giggle at the thought of animals and could not imagine what kind of animals anyone would want or what they would do with them. Several times her eyes went back to the words gang bang. She wondered how many men and what it would feel like to have several men at the same time. She closed the brochure still torn between fulfilling her sexual desires and just having a normal vacation or both. The dream about her father was perhaps an omen of sorts she thought. He was always so conservative, so reserved. She couldn't remember her mother and father ever kissing or so much as holding hands. In high school other classmates had remarked about catching their parents having sex but she never did. She just assumed they didn't have sex and now she wondered what that must had been like for her mother, the lack of intimacy, the lack of sexual satisfaction because she couldn't imagine her mother satisfying herself.

Marilyn finally decided to take it slow, for now, she was interested in horse back riding. When her father was stationed in Virginia they were very close to a stable. She would ride a couple times a week. Each activity in the brochure had a number code so she just picked up the phone and dialed a number and punched in the code.

At the stable she was a little disappointed that the three horses they had were old geldings because she wanted a younger horse that could gallop but she figured most of the guests preferred a more lesirley ride. It took several mintues and saddeling the horse herself to convince the stable hands that she was an experienced rider. They suggested that the race track would have a horse she could take one around the track for a few laps. She was trying to remember that she was on vacation to have fun but the accountant in her kept telling her that things like that were very expensive and were for the rich and famous and not for people like her. She took the youngest of the three and they provided water and a picnic lunch. It was good to be on a horse again to have all that power, all that beastly power, between her legs. But it was different this time, different from when she was a teenager and she now realized that all the horseback riding had fulfilled a young girl's need for some stimulation between her legs. As the horse made its way down the trail with little guidance, she got into the rhythm of its movement but unlike when she was young it was not enough movement to satisfy any craving. The trail went though the woods and there were beautiful arrays of flowers. In a couple places, where the path widened, she tried to get the horse to move faster but it was stuck in its routine. Finally she found a clearing with some shade and she now wished she had bought the hat Leslie had recommended. As she shared her lunch with the horse she thought about Leslie and what kind of relationship she could have with her. Of course she knew about lesbians and wondered if that what she would be if she had a constant relationship with her and would she like that? Would they live together or would they just see each other occasionally? All these things were going through her mind because now there was a vacuum that normally would be filled with thoughts about work. As she lay down in the grass she tried to clear her mind but images of her and Leslie together kept flooding into her mind. Leslie excited her so much, loved to dominate her but what kind of relationship was that certainly not a normal one like a boyfriend or husband the kind of relationship she grew up thinking was normal. More images flooded into her mind of her pert, full, pierced breasts. Her chains glistened in her mind and before she realized it her hand was in her slacks finding that spot that bought so much pleasure. Suddenly there were noises and she quickly got to her feet. A man and woman rode up the path. They talked briefly and were a married couple on holiday from Dallas. They both had Spanish accents and perfect tans. The woman told her she was getting slightly red so Marilyn mounted up and headed back to the stables. Leslie was right it didn't take long here for the sun to do damage.

After returning the horse she stopped at the main building. It was lavishly furnished in a jungle motif. A large stone fireplace was on one wall. In the back was a large pool surrounded by palm trees. There were three clerks behind the desk busily waiting on other gustes who were just arriving and taking phone calls. When she got their attention, she asked for Gerald to get more information on the scuba diving.

"I am very sorry Miss Winters but Gerald has been reassigned to another guest. I am very sorry for an inconvience. I will have Clark here in just a minute."

All Marilyn could do was smile because she had a pretty good idea who had requested him. Clark was another tall, thin, good looking young man. He explained diving in great detail and then arranged for a two hour lesson in the morning and half a day of diving in the afternoon. On a whim Marilyn went to the commissary and bought supper and breakfast deciding to cook something she did very little of at home. When she got back to villa it was early evening and she couldn't believe how fast the first day had gone. For awhile, she was afraid that she was going to have to call Clark to help her with the grill on the deck but finally figured it out but wondered if she had called him and he came over could she seduce him. It would be like having sex with a complete stranger. She was just as much a novice with sex as she was with cooking. She had never been picked up in a bar nor had casual sex with anyone. She knew people did it all the time but she had never been interested but she was interested now.

The second chicken breast was a little overly done but she ate it anyway. She sat in the lounge chair and watched the sunset and it was beautiful orange, red, and purple, streaked across the sky. When she got up, her muscles were stiff and sore. It had been years since those muscles had been used. There was a whirlpool bathtub but what she really needed was a massage. Marilyn was still trying to decide what to wear when she heard the doorbell. She had never received a full body massage at a hotel before the ones in the past were just done to relieve tension and done while she was fully dressed.

Finally she just through on a pair of shorts and a big top and ran to the door.

"Good evening Madam."

He had an accent. Perhaps it was French but she wasn't sure, at least European. He came in carrying a table and a large gym back. He set up the table.

"You are must to modest Madam," he said as he held up two small towels. Marilyn wasn't sure if she was to get undressed right there or go into the bathroom. When he turned around to get oil out of his bag she quickly slipped off the top and shorts.

"Should I be on my front or back," she asked and trying in vain to cover herself with the towels.

"Which ever way is more comfortable? Where are you feeling the most discomfort?"

"My legs, my thighs, and hips."

"Then lay on your stomach."

She put her face in the cut out in the table. She tried to cover her bottom with the towel but it was too small. He arraigned the towel so it covered most of it and then started on her lower back. His fingers were strong and firm. He worked the lower back and then massaged her upper thighs.

"You have several knots her Madam," he said as he worked on the thighs. Marilyn was melting into the table fighting the urge to moan, trying to keep her breathing normal. He worked her muscles like a musical insterment and what came out was all the soreness. After putting some more oil on his hands, he started on the thighs again but in a few moments he was massaging her sensitive inner thigh and Marilyn, despite her best efforts, let out a large moan. In a moment the massage had changed from physical to sensual. He took off the towel and massaged her cheeks.

"Yes, very nice," he said as he ran his fingers between them.

Marilyn was breathing hard and moaning and she didn't care. She was sure that she had punched in the code for a regular massage and not the sexual massage but she didn't care about that either. He spread her cheeks with his thumbs and then massaged each one. He poured oil on the very top and she felt it flow down and between her cheeks and she thought it was wonderful. He started at the top and did her neck and shoulders and massaged everything even the balls of her feet. Marilyn was in a state of total euphoria when she heard him say, "Do you have a preference Madam."

She lifted up her head and he was holding a case with four dildos inside. One was very small and made of a shinny silver metal, one was large and pink and looked like rubber, one was blue and curved at the tip, and one was crystal with ridges. She touched the crystal one. She jumped when the tip touched her.

"Are you a virgin, Madame?"

"No," she replied quickly. She spread her legs until her knees were over the side of the table, got up and rested on her forearms.

"Now do me."

She knew that it was the point of no return. She had to have it. And was starting to believe that she could never go back to being that person who was the workalochol without a sex life; she craved it; she needed it.

He worked it in slow but firm and then out again and then kept up a nice steady pace. He massaged her cheeks.

"Yes do me there too."

"What would you like Madam?"

She had thought about it but had never said the words not even to Leslie.

"Do my ass."

"Are you sure Madam?"

"Damn it, do my ass."

He slid the thin vibrator into her and she loved it, she loved the feeling of both of them inside of her. She loved being in that zone, being in control.

"That's it ram it into me, do me damn it, do me, yes, yes, do me damn it." She now liked the sounds of the dirty words and knowing he would do anything she commanded. She started giving him specific orders telling just where and how fast to do it until she reached that state she craved, the state of continous orgasms.

She hadn't slept that late in years, called up and cancelled the scuba diving. Now, that other side of her had been awakened and had to me satisfied but she had to be patient because it to be dark out. She took a swim in the ocean making sure not to go out to deep. Even though she had been on the swimming team both in high school and college the undercurrents were powerful and dangerous. Then she took a long bath and watched another beautiful sunset and then called the number. She turned off all the lights, lit two candles placing them by the bed, and got totally naked. When the door bell rang she went to the door naked, ready. There were four of them; two of them looked a little ruff with tattoos on their arms. They picked her up, carrying her, and threw her on the bed. Two of them grabbed her ankles and spread her legs wide. One of them took off he pants and shirt and got between her legs. She knew for sure that she had never been this excited before. He pushed in and then stopped.

"You're really tight."

"Then do me and open me up."

One of them offered his manhood and she gladly took into her mouth. This night she wanted to be a total slut. The other one offered his and she went from one to the other while the fourth one just stood at the edge of the bed watching. They each took their turn and she loved it, becoming a conisour of her own orgasm judging each one by its strength and duration. She never knew sex could be so intoxicating and was getting high on the smell of their sweat and sex. The fourth one just stood watching as the other three had her from the front and while she was on her hands and knees. She thought it couldn't get any more perfect as two of them sucked on her nipples while one pumped in and out of her when the fourth finally took off his shirt and slowly removed his pants. Even in the dim candlelight she could tell he was huge, hanging almost down to his knees. He got on top of the bed and stroked himself and she had no idea that anyone could be that big.

"Are sure you want it."

"Yes, yes, do me with that monster."

She never felt so full brought up her long legs and wrapped them around his shoulders.

"I guess you really want it," he said, kissing her neck.

"I'm a slut, so do me good."

He got on his knees, grabbed the back of her head and started pumping in and out. Marilyn felt her insides expand with his massive tool and for the first time she felt her juice squirt and squirt. He did her until she arched her back, screamed, and collapsed on the bed.

They were all spread out on the bed and Marilyn thought the smell and sounds of their sex was the most beautiful thing in the world.

"Are you satisfied now lady?"

"I'm afraid that I'm insatiable.

She got on her hands and knees.

"Now you can start doing my ass."

"That's it lady, now you are really going to get it you slut."

The three of them did all her holes as she barked orders at them. He got his massive tool completely hard again. They picked her up and lowered her down on him. His tool scraped her insides and she rode him like she had fantasized, bucked on him, slammed herself down on him and when he went soft she still kept bucking up against his half hard member until she collapsed from sheer exhaustion but with a continuous orgasm.

When she awoke they were gone. The smell of their sex was still in the air and her insides were throbbing. It is all over now, she thought. She had satisfied her carnel lust and now she could go back to her old life.

XIV

The scuba gear was heavy but once in the water she felt free. Her powerful legs moved her through the water with ease. And the world below was beautiful. There were fish of very color and description and she especially like the rays, the way they glided through the water and would bury themselves using the sand for camouflage.

Back at the villa she was surprised that the phone was blinking with a message. It was Abby asking her to come to her villa. She told her to go to the front desk and ask for Ramos. Marilyn wasn't sure if she was up to a night of girl talk. She was surprised how a few hours in the sun or the sea could make a person tired but she liked Abby and a chance to spend more time with her favorite soap opera star was something she couldn't pass up so after supper she took a quick nap so she would be fresh for a long night of girl talk.

During supper she noticed on the events calendar that it was also the night for the guest get together at the pool and decided to do both. The black dress that Leslie had picked out was backless and had a deep cut in the front. Self consiuses about her lack of cleavage she tied a scarf around her neck that fell down and covered most of the front.

In the pool area she was surprised how few people there were counting only seven, figuring most of the guests preferred their privacy. She noticed that a dark haired man was looking at her, more like staring, at her as she walked the length of the pool and up to the bar. She ordered a gin and tonic and just took her first sip when she heard.

"Come over and join us," a woman's voice said and Marilyn recognized the couple from the airport.

Marilyn went over to their table, sat down, and then realized that the dress was very short exposing much of her slightly red, upper thigh.

"My name is Beverly and this is my husband Harold."

"It's nice to meet you."

"Are you having fun," she asked.

"Yes, it's very nice."

"So where are you from?" Harold asked.

"New York."

"I was their once, I didn't like it, too many people, too noisy."
Marilyn only smiled.

"So what do you do there? I own fourteen hardware stores in
Kansas City and St. Louis."

"I work on wall street, mergers and acquisitions."

"Big corporate stuff so what are you into down her?"

"Harold, please, it is none of our business."

"Let me tell you this is our third trip down here and these
people will do anything you want if you know what I mean, anything.
At our age we can't do each other like we used to so we come down
here."

"Please, Harold you are embarsing the poor girl."

"There's nothing to be embarrassed about we all know why we
come here." Harold belched and then said, "I need another beer. Do
you want anything?"

"No thank you," Marilyn replied.

"I have to apologize for Harold he can be such a cad. He was
much more romantic when we were younger. Now he just wants to
hurry up and get it over with. The truth is I come down here to be
romanced. Of course, Harold thinks that I'm in to some kinky sex
thing but I just like to have some romance."

"I understand," Marilyn replied. She noticed Harold was
coming back.

"It was nice meeting you, but I think that I will mingle."

"I understand dear."

The dark haired man was staring at her again as she made her
way to the bar. She ordered another gin and tonic. When she turned
around he was gone. She made small talk with some of the guests as she
made her way to the other side of the pool. Most were single and this
was their first time at the resort. She was looking at the pool when she
heard from behind her, "Do you swim, Marilyn."

"Yes, I was state champion three years."

"I would like to see you swim." It was the dark haired man. "You're very tall, that's good." The top of his head just came up to her nose.

He circled her, looking her over, inspecting her.

"If you worked out and put on ten pounds of muscle you would be very formidable. I'm not talking like a body builder just toned and buffed.

"How do you know my name?"

"Here is my card, Leslie told me about you."

She looked at the card and it said David Wells, President, All Star Entertainment and a phone number.

"And how do you know Leslie?" Marilyn wondered as she asked the question why she would feel a bit jealous.

"We refer clients to each other. She told me about you."

He grabbed her gently by the arm and led her over to a table and chairs. Marilyn sat down letting her dress ride up. She wanted him to see her legs.

"I have a dominatrix that is about to take some time off and I need a replacement."

"A what?"

"People will pay to have you dominate them sexually men and women."

Marilyn was stunned that not only Leslie had told someone how she dominated her but something like that would be a job, a way to make a living.

"How much are we talking about?"

"Our clients will pay up to one thousand in which one third is yours."

"You mean one half."

David grinned. "Leslie said you would be a tough negotiator."

"I say one third until you can prove you can retain the current clients and then it will be one half."

"How many clients a day?"

"That's up to you, two or three."

She did the calculations quickly and she could make almost as much money in year as she was getting now but it was more than the money. Just the thought of getting paid, having a job performing sex excited her, made her feel alive.

"Leslie said you would want do your research. On the back of the card is the woman's name and phone number you would be replacing. When you get back to New York give her call. She will be happy to show you the ropes."

He stood up and put his hand on her shoulder. "I think it would be good for you. I think you would really enjoy it. You will have to excuse me now I have to check on some of my clients."

She looked at the card for a few moments. It was ludicrous, a mere fantasy and besides she was putting all that behind her and getting back to a normal life.

XV

After driving down three different roads the driver pulled up and stopped in front of a chain stretched across the road. A sign saying private hung from the chain. As they drove on the road turned into a lane that was just wide enough for one vehicle. They pulled up into a large circle drive and in front of the largest villa on the resort a four bedroom estate. The servants stayed at the villa when it was occupied. That day, Abbey had dismissed all the women servants, all nine of them. None of them met her needs. Abbey answered the door wearing pajamas and with her hair in pigtails trying very had to look like a little girl.

"You look very nice. That dress looks good on you."

"I think it's a little too short."

"Nonsense, you really have the legs for it."

Abby sat of the couch and patted the seat for her to sit next to her. Marilyn sat down and Abby moved even closer."

"Are you enjoying your vacation?" Abby asked.

"Yes, it's been wonderful."

"I lied on the plane," Abby said as she put her small hand on Marilyn's knee and then ran it up her leg and underneath her dress.

"I don't come here to be romanced, I come here to have sex with women," she said as her hand found the bottom of Marilyn's panties and then found her inner thigh. Marilyn spread her legs just a little giving her a little more access but not too much. She wanted to tease her.

"I saw the way you looked at me on the plane. I could tell you were interested. I can tell the way one woman looks at another."

"But you've been married four times."

"Yes, just long enough for them to figure out I prefer woman. It's been that way all my life. Hollywood has such a double standard,"

Abby said as she tried to get her hands between her legs but Marilyn pressed her legs together cutting her off.

Marilyn bent down and kissed her gently. She couldn't believe this beautiful woman wanted her and she was getting that sexual high again. Marilyn ran her hand over her cheek, down her neck, until she reached the top button of her pajamas and then she pulled popping the button. Abby gasped and her breathing was irractic.

"Why would you want me when all you have to do is pick up the phone and they will bring what you want," Marilyn said as she popped the second button.

"You are not a paid service."

"Would you pay for me if you had to," she said as she popped another button.

"Yes, I would pay what ever you want."

Marilyn reached in and found her pert, little breasts, surprised on how small they were because on the show all the outfits she wore made her look well endowed. She massaged it, finding the nipple squeezing it between her finger and thumb. Abby was breathing hard. Marilyn noticed her hand was in her pajama bottoms. She grabbed her wrist and pulling her hand away taking away her pleasure.

"Not yet, I will tell you when you deserve it."

"Yes, mother."

Marilyn took her cue, knew now what she wanted, and she wanted it too. She removed the straps of her dress exposing her breasts.

"Suck mommy's tit."

Abby found her large, engorged nipple and sucked on it like a baby.

"You have such big, delisous nipples," then Abby took it between her lips and massaged it.

Marilyn reached into her pajama bottoms and found her spot and massaged it like they taught her and Abby's body shook with pleasure. Abby bit down on her nipple and Marilyn jumped. Marilyn grabbed the back of her hair and pushed her over her lap.

"You are a bad little girl."

"Yes, mother. I've been very bad."

Marilyn pulled down her pajama bottoms exposing her small, white cheeks. She ran her fingers between them and then brought her hand down hard. She brought her hand down hard several more times, liked the way her cheeks vibrated and shook from the force.

"Now suck my nipples."

She did and bit down again.

"You are a bad, bad, little girl. You need to be really punished; we need to find a belt."

"No mommy, not the belt."

Marilyn dragged her into the bedroom by the hair, rummaged through her closet until she found a thin black belt. She folded it over and snapped it. Marilyn removed her dress and panties then snapped the belt again.

"You know what you have to do."

Abby pushed down her pajama bottoms with trebling hands. Marilyn let her please herself as she whipped her. Abby cried out from the pain and pleasure.

Marilyn finally dropped the belt, got on the bed, and spread her legs wide.

"Now come here and please mommy and do it good or you will be punished again."

Abby's whole body was trembling. Marilyn found her to be adequate but not like Leslie who could be gentle have her totally relaxed and floating or in just a few moments bring her to the edge of escatcy then back down again or quickly push her over the edge at her will. Marilyn let her please herself as she was serviced.

"And what about Gerald?" Marilyn asked after several orgasms.

"He just makes sure that I have the right staff, young, pretty woman."

"That you try and seduce"

"Yes."

"Like you seduced me."

"Yes, it's so exciting."

"Do they punish you?"

"Yes, if I'm lucky. Please spend the night and punish me in the morning."

In the morning Marilyn tied her to the shower, curtain rod and whipped her before they took a shower together and pleased each other.

As the jeep roared down the road taking her back to her villa, her hair blowing in the wind, she was amazed how people craved different sexual activities but still had no idea that she was just scratching the surface to the diversity of human sexual desire.

Even though Marilyn was a two sport athletele in high school, playing basketball, and swimming, she was terrible at golf. The ball was going everywhere except where she wanted it to go. She spent too much time in the sun, again, after playing just eight holes. So she decided to stick to something that she knew best, swimming. Down at the beach she found young couples were streached out on towels, totally naked, even some of the older couples were doing it. Marilyn had enough of the sun so she laid out her towel and dove into the ocean.

As she was drying herself off and enjoying that refreshing feeling after a good swim a young man, at least ten years younger, came over.

"I was watching you swim, you are very good."

"Thank you."

"I saw you at the pool when you were diving, very impressive."

Marilyn wasn't trying to show off it was just something she had done since she was a little girl.

"Oh, it wasn't that good; I'm really out of shape."

"You look in shape to me."

He laid out his towel and sat next to her and Marilyn was thankful he wasn't one of the nude sun bathers. She really did not want to deal with that.

"You know," he said, "there is a dinner cruse aboard a yacht tonight. It's one of those things you would like to do but don't want to go alone. So, if you are interested we could go together."

"Sure, why not," Marilyn responded.

"Great, I will meet you at the dock."

He got up quickly and headed to wear the nude sun bathers were gathered.

They met at the dock and boarded together. As the yacht pulled out the sun was just beginning to set. From the ocean one could see just how isolated some of the villa's were and Marilyn wondered which one was Abby's. They talked briefly about their work and where they came from while the sun set and the yaht headed farther out to sea. He was president of an electronics manufacturing company and heard about the resort from a sales rep. A waiter came out and told them that dinner was being served. They went inside and Marilyn ordered a double gin and tonic because she felt very nervous. Each table was a window seat and they brought out sea bass with potatoes.

"So, have you tried any of their other services here, I don't mean to pry. I'm just curious?" he asked.

"Yes, I'm just experimenting," Marilyn replied but she really didn't want to talk about it.

"I know what you mean. Just between you and me I thought that it would be like being a kid in a candy store but the novelty kind of wears off after the first couple of days. I guess that I'm looking more for a relationship. I should have gone on one of those single cruses."

A small band started playing cilopseo music. He finished the dinner in record time, excused himself and went to the dance floor and started talking to a couple of young women who were dancing with each other. Marilyn slowly ate her dinner, finished her drink and ordered another double.

She walked out on to the outer deck. The yacht had slowed but it was moving fast enough to create a pleasant breeze. The full moon was out and the ocean was clam and peaceful. Men were just not interested, Marilyn thought, young, old, it didn't make a difference. She now wished that she had never felt an orgasm, it had consumed her, taken over her life. She wished that she could go back before she ever heard of Avalon.

XVI

As the resort disappeared in the distance, she was already forming a plan. Without the day planner she was busy writing notes on the resort stationary. By the time the plane touched down at home she would have a plan to get back to her old life. Each day would be planned. There would be daily and weekly goals. She would make partner in six months, break off all contact with Avalon and Leslie. She wrote: fire Jason, and circled it, to reestablish her control right away. But she wished he would service her before he left but dismissed that thought very quickly and was determined to quickly dismiss all those kinds of thoughts. Now it would be impossible to completely eliminate all those kinds of thoughts but if she dismissed them as quickly as they came she could keep her focus.

She started to straighten out her purse, a compulsive habit she had picked up and found David's card. She wondered why she hadn't thrown it away at the resort. Did it mean something? Did it mean that she still wasn't sure of her direction? Then she decided it was out of habit. She never threw away a business card: there was a drawer full of cards in her office kept them because you never knew when you might need a contact. She would file it with the other cards and that would be the end of it.

As she put away her clothes a little jet lag was settling in. With two more days off, she planned to start first thing in the morning after a good nights sleep but then the phone rang.

"Good evening, it's Leslie from Avalon. I hope your vacation was satisfactory."

"Yes, it was wonderful."

"I hope our service met your expectations."

"Yes, everything was fine."

"I have a short customer satisfaction questionnaire we like our first time guests to complete. Perhaps I could bring-'

"Have it sent my office and I will complete it."

"Would you like to set up an appointment with us?"

"No, not at this time I will be in touch if I require your services in the future. Thank you very much." She hung up and thinking that she handled that perfectly, broken off all ties in a professional like manner.

She called Patricia and talked to for over an hour giving the details of her vacation but leaving out any thing of a sexual nature. She told her about the horse back riding, the scuba diving, the swimming and how she had wished they had a three meter board at the pool but there still was a few people watching and clapping as she did her diving routine. Told her that she met Abby on the plane just briefly but left everything else out. When Patricia asked if she took advantage of any of the sexual services the only thing Marilyn would say was that it was a normal vacation. She was satisfied now and soon all of it would become a distant memory.

She was just coming out of the bathroom, drying her hair, when the door bell rang. She couldn't imagine who it could it be and gasped when she looked through the peep hole and saw Leslie. She was wearing a cobalt blue business suite with a ruffled shirt with a bow around her neck, very professional. Marilyn thought she could let her in and dismiss her in a professional like manner and then it would be over even though it was going to be hard to be professional in a bathrobe.

"I just wanted to delivery the questionnaire in person. On the phone I got the impression that you were dissatisfied with our service."

Marilyn took the questionnaire and threw it on the coffee table. She sat on the couch and pulled the bathroom tightly trying to cover as much as possible.

"Your service was excellent. It's just that I won't need your service anymore."

"I see," Leslie said as she unbuttoned her jacket and let it fall to the floor. She undid her bow and let it fall to the floor. Everything was happing in slow motion for Marilyn. All she could think of was please no, I can't, but she was mesmerized, transfixed. Leslie unbuttoned her blouse exposing the leather collar around her neck. She took off her blouse exposing her chains. Marilyn couldn't say anything. Leslie turned around showing her that a thin leather strap went down from the collar and then she removed her skirt letting her see the strap went between her cheeks. Then turned and showed her that the strap went between her legs and was attached to the clit ring.

"That's what I had to do to keep from thinking about you. Maybe you don't need Avalon anymore. But does that mean you don't need me too?"

Marilyn reached out and grabbed the chains pulling her close burying her face between her breasts and licking her skin. She ran her hands all over her body and breathed in deeply and was once again intoxicated by the feel and smell of her body.

She undid the leather strap from the clit ring.

"Oh, please."

Marilyn kissed her deeply and then gently bit her lower lip."

"Please, what?"

"Please abuse me?"

Marilyn pulled up on the leather strap.

"Oh, yes, that's it, pull it hard."

Marilyn jerked on it hard several times and then kept pulling up as she removed one of her chains, removed her nipple ring and sucked and chewed on her nipple. Leslie's body shook from the force of her orgasm.

Marilyn unhooked the strap from her collar.

"Oh, please don't"

"Shhh," Marilyn said as she stood up. "I'm in control now."

She worked the strap back and forth letting it dig into her.

"Oh, please don't stop, it really hurts."

Marilyn grabbed the back of her hair, pulled her head back, and forced her tongue into her mouth. When they broke their long kiss Marilyn dug her finger nails into her breast.

"I'm going to take you into the bedroom and abuse you and when I'm done you will service me."

"Yes, please, I love you too."

Marilyn took her into the bedroom and whipped her with the leather strap and then they brought each other to complete ecstasy over and over again. And when they were laying together and Marilyn was enjoying the feel of her body and the smell of their sex she knew one life was defiantly over but not the one she had planned on.

XVII

When Marilyn arrived David was there to great her. He showed her around his stable as he put it. It was a small stable. There was Marge who looked like she should still be in grade school who took care of the older male clients. She even had one that was in his nineties. Then there was Johnny who specialized in sexual massages with mostly woman clients but there were also a couple of men. And then there was Pricilla, a quick change artist. Like her mother, she could go from looking like a cow girl to a nun in moments. Her mother's act was the stuff of legends in Las Vegas. Finally David led Marilyn down a narrow hallway and into a large, dark room. It was nothing like Avalon with its fountains and lavish furniture. This place was dark and gritty. It was just two blocks away from the hookers and the adult books. It was an old movie theater. The movie marquee was gone the door and windows were painted black.

Clients had to have a key to enter and the entrance was monitored by surveillance cameras. Special movies were still shown for special clients, films that were illegal in some countries. The adjacent building, once a drug store, was turned into performance rooms.

"You can wait for Stephanie in here," said Jimmy, a young, thin boy, with a pencil behind his ear and carrying a clipboard where he kept track of all the clients and staff.

She looked at the costumes. There was maid outfit, a cheerleading outfit, a nurse's uniform, and a nun's outfit with cross. She touched and different restraints as she made her way around the room. In the center were two large dressing tables with mirrors. Near the back was a bed. She picked up a leather device and couldn't imagine where it would be used on the human body or for what purpose. Through the walls she could just make out the cracking of a whip and moaning.

A door in the back of the room opened up and in came a woman wearing dark stockings, a corset, that made her breasts bulge at the top, and she was carrying a whip.

"You must be Marilyn."

"Yes, it's nice to meet you."

Marilyn felt out of place in her dark business suite but didn't know what else to wear. This was not like any other interview she had been on.

"David told me you're an uptown girl."

"Yes, I work on wall street."

Stephanie hung her whip over the chair and picked up a towel and wiped the sweat that glistened on her chest and arms. Marilyn noticed right away how powerful she looked with strong looking shoulders, arms and legs but she also noticed that she was just beginning to show. She had seen enough of her aunts growing up and woman in her office building to know it had to be several months.

She lit up a cigarette.

"I know it's a bad habit."

"Especially someone in your condition."

"Does it show that much?"

"Only another woman would notice right now. Does David know?"

"No, he's clueless. Just bring in the money and he's happy. I suppose even he will notice pretty soon. Have you ever dominated anyone sexually?"

"Yes."

"And did you enjoy it."

"Yes."

"Well this job isn't about your pleasure. It's about satisfying the client. It's not like any other job. You please the client and you get paid. Don't please the clients and you won't last a week. Men and women will pay you to dominate them. Each one wants something different. Some you can dominate with just your voice and how you present yourself. Others you have to be physical with and use restraints. Again it's about pleasing your clients. Some of them you have to know what they want because they won't tell you. Others will tell you want they want but you still have to be in charge. They are paying you to be in control."

She got up grabbed the whip and made it crack. Marilyn jumped.

"Have you ever used a whip?"

"No."

"I can teach you that." She cracked the whip again.

"Now take your clothes off." Marilyn quickly started taking her clothes off.

"You never touch a client with the whip. The sound gets them off."

Marilyn could not believe she was standing before this woman in just her panties and bra.

"Why did you take off your clothes?" You took them off because I commanded you and you obeyed. You have to learn how to use your voice to give commands to make the client obey because that's what they want."

She circled Marilyn, inspecting her. "You're a little soft. Some buffing in the gym will fix that. The arms and shoulders have to be strong but the key is in the legs. You don't look bad you must have been an athlete. Take off your panties"

Marilyn slid them down and she grabbed her ass.

"Yes, very nice. Defiantly your best feature, that and your powerful looking thighs."

Without being told Marilyn took off the bra.

Stephanie came around front and took out the breast forms that made her breasts bulge.

"Honey, you're going to need a couple of these because men and women like to see some cleavage."

She went and dug through a number of outfits and brought out a small, black corset.

"From my younger, thinner days."

Marilyn put on the corset and then inserted the breast forms and then Stephanie cinched her, looking her up and down. Marilyn couldn't believe that even she had cleavage now.

She put on fish net stockings and a pair of shoes with six inch, spike heels.

"Now sit in the chair."

Stephanie frizzed her hair and applied dark eye shadow and dark lipstick.

"Now come stand in front of the mirror. "

Marilyn looked at herself in the full length mirror, saw power, felt excitement.

"Does it excite you?" Marilyn asked.

"Of course, I wouldn't do it if it didn't excite me. But like I said it's not about your excitement it's about pleasing the client. If you get off on it that's a bonus."

Stephanie inspected her in the mirror. "A little buffing and you would be perfect. Mistress Marilyn. Madame Marilyn. It does have a ring to it."

She reached between her legs and touched her. "You need to shave down there, just the sides; you can leave a little bush at the top." Stephanie ran her fingers between her cheeks and then massaged her ass. Marilyn loved the way she looked. She like the power she represented.

"You're a good looking dominatrix."

"Do they want to have sex with you?" Marilyn asked.

"No, most of them never touch you. There is only one that I've ever done it with."

"Is that how you got pregnant?"

"Yes, but I wanted to get pregnant. I've always wanted a child. I know that I'm old but women my age have children all the time. I picked someone from good breading stock if you know what I mean."

"You won't do this afterwards?"

"No, I'm done. I have got a couple of clients I may keep just because they are special. I ran away from home when I was thirteen and started doing tricks at fourteen but I never let the pimps take advantage of me or push me around like some of the girls. My mother was a tramp and we moved around a lot. When she got drunk she would beat me so I took off. I was totally out of control when I was younger, sex, and drugs. But I got off the street and did escort service for a time and then this. I bet your childhood was much different. I bet you grew up in the suburbs, probably boarding school or private school."

"My father was in the military so we moved around a lot. I went to public schools but we always had a nice house in nice neighborhoods."

"That's what I want for my daughter."

"Or son."

"Or son. A stable home life, something they can count on."

"Can you afford to retire?"

"I've always watched my money. I bet that I was the only hooker on the street with a savings account. I made almost a hundred thousand last year because I do things that David doesn't know about."

"How many clients do you see a day."

"Just two now but I used to do three or four a day when I started. You can see as many as you want and you can make as much money as you want but somehow I don't think you are doing this for the money."

"No, I want a job that excites me."

"Your current job doesn't excite you?"

"No, I took it to impress my father but now I want to do something for me. What kind of clients do you have?"

"I have both men and women. Some I know maybe too well. Others I have no idea who they are. They wear masks. It's just as much for my protection as it is for theirs."

"When will my training start?"

"I want you to go home and think about it and I mean really think about it. This is a big change for a woman like you. On Monday, if you are still interested, you call me and we will get started."

"Can I keep the outfit for now?"

"For a special friend?"

"Yes, and could I borrower some restraints and a few other things."

Stephanie gave her a pair of handcuffs and showed how easy they were to use and then showed her how to grab a person's thumb and make them do just about anything you wanted.

After she got to her office and made sure no one was working, she called Patricia and told her to come to her office and then they would go out to dinner. Marilyn put on the outfit that she now called her battle gear. She shut all the drapes, turned off all the lights except for the bathroom that cast just a little light in the office, and then she sat down in her office chair and waited for her victim. She was so excited that she had to touch herself and please herself. Finally after what seemed like an eternity to Marilyn, the office door opened.

"Why is it so dark in her? Why have you got all the lights turned off?"

Marilyn stood up and stepped into the light.

"Marilyn is that you? What did you do?" Oh my, you're gorgeous."

Marilyn circled her very close so she could see her pushed up breasts close up then got behind her, pushed her hair out of the way, and kissed her neck. Patricia started to moan. It even surprised Marilyn how quickly and easily it was to put the handcuffs on. She pulled up on them and pushed her over to the coffee table where she had spread out her other items. She pulled up harder and she went down on her knees.

"What are going to do to me?" Patricia asked when saw the riding crop and dildo.

"Shhh, Marilyn whispered into her ear then she sucked on her ear and neck bringing her back under her sexual control. Marilyn ripped open her blouse, reached into her bra and brought out one her massive breasts. She reached in and lifted out the other, massaged them and sucked on her neck until she was moaning again and then she quickly picked up the riding crop and brought it down on her breasts making Patricia cry out in pain. Marilyn sucked on her ear. "You've never really satisfied me but you are going to satisfy me now."

Marilyn picked up the dildo and pushed it between her breasts so she could feel how large and firm it was.

"If you please me, I will do you with this. But if you don't please me, you will get this." Marilyn said as she ran the rough handle of the riding crop between her breasts.

Using the handcuffs she make her bend over until her breasts were on the coffee table then pulled up her skirt, pulled on her pantyhose until they ripped away from her body. She brought the riding crop down across her flabby ass.

"Please Marilyn, please stop."

She brought the riding crop down on her again.

"You're not saying what I want to hear."

"Please, let me satisfy you," Patricia pleaded as she pushed the handle of the riding crop between her cheeks. Marilyn reached in between her legs and found her wetness.

"What a slut, you came already didn't you?"

"I'm sorry, I couldn't help it."

Marilyn pushed the handle of the riding crop between her cheeks until the tip pressed against her opening.

"Please, please, not there, not with that." Patricia tried to break free but she was pulling up on the handcuffs keeping her pinned to the table.

"I should really ream you out with this. You don't dare come before I do. Do you understand me?"

"Yes, yes, I'm so very sorry; let me make it up to you."

Just for good measure she brought the riding crop down across her ass again but with a lighter hand this time. Grabbing her by the hair she pulled over the coffee table. Marilyn sat on the back of the couch and spread her legs.

"So, start pleasing me or I will," she said as she raised the riding crop up.

Patricia went right for her inner thighs and sucked on them and then worked her way to where Marilyn needed it the most. She was trying very hard but she wasn't giving Marilyn what she craved so she started barking orders at her telling her just what to do with her tongue and lips. Finally, Marilyn could feel it build inside of her and start to roll through her like a wave, a wave of escatcy. Marilyn held her head.

"Now eat my juice you bitch." And she did.

"Are you satisfied now?" Patricia asked.

"You are just getting started," Marilyn said as she brought the riding crop down across her back letting her know that she was still in charge.

"Don't worry, it will get easier." And it did because she was now in complete control. After filling her mouth three more times with juice, she pushed her down on the couch and worked the dildo in and out of her as she massaged her breasts.

"I've always liked these," Marilyn said. She liked the way they overflowed in her hand. "I see the way men and women look at you. I'm so jealous. I wish that mine was that big."

"Can I come now," Patricia asked politely.

"Yes, you can come now."

"Thank you." Marilyn felt her body shake.

"I'm sorry I never satisfied you. I will try harder in the future. We have to do this again."

"Next time you will pay me," Marilyn replied as she kissed her cheek.

"I will pay what ever you want."

XVIII

Resigning was easier then she thought it would be. Jason was like a kid in a candy store with his new promotion and authority. She wanted to drag the little twit into a conference room or store room and make him service her but fought off the temptation all the way to her last day where there was large going away party and she drank way too much.

Her mother finally tracked her down after a week and she told her that she would be a consultant to people who were interested in buying a business or property for a tax shelter.

She met with David and made him put the terms of her employment in writing. Something he had never done before. Her portfolio was in good shape and with the company stock options and company bonus she could live for several years without working at all so she told David to buy health insurance for Stephanie and to take it out of her check. David informed her that this was a cash business and what she reported to the tax man was her business so Marilyn got the policy herself and paid the first three years in advance. He had no idea why she would want to do something like that and she couldn't believe that he still didn't know that Stephanie was pregnant.

Patricia became her first client with a standing appointment every Friday night. She called Leslie three times but she was always busy so she finally left a message telling her how sorry she was that she was taking a client away from her but it was business. Marilyn hit the gym in the daytime, downing protein shakes to bulk up and working with free weights to build up her shoulders and arms. At night, Stephanie schooled her in the use of the whip, how to bring it so close they could feel the air rushing by them but not hitting them. She took a hit to her own leg and thigh before she got the hang of it. She also got schooled in the use of restraints, how to tell if they were too tight by the color of the skin because the clients were too excited to judge if it was cutting off their circulation, learned how to suspend a two hundred and fifty pound man with the use of pulleys with out putting too much pressure on his joints and tendons. She found out, like her old job, clients came by word of mouth but it was much more subdued. Companies wanted to keep possible mergers or acquitions quite as long as possible. Now she was working in something people didn't talk about in public something that a person would maybe not even tell their best friend and for a lot people it was less socially acceptable than alcoholism or drug abuse. So the clients could only be referred by another member of this subculture and then accepted only after a background check. Clients were never referred to by name but by nickname. There was never a paper trail that could lead back to the client.

After a week Marilyn had not heard from Leslie so she called her office from a pay phone and left a message telling that she missed her and to please contact her. The cell phone was gone because they could be traced by anyone with the desire and the right equipment. No day planner because even coded notes could be broken. All contact with the client was in person or though only one trusted intermediary.

Marilyn was not completely surprised when Leslie was waiting for her when she got home. Coming home every night was a new experience for her but she still was still in training. Leslie was wearing the tightest pair of jeans and that low cut top that Marilyn liked so much.

"Do you like your new job?"

"Yes, I like it very much but I'm still in training."

"I haven't heard from you for awhile so I was just wondering," Marilyn said. She was still unsure of their relationship, were they lovers? Or was it just a business relationship with out the fees?

"I've been very busy trying to recruit new clients. I lost two clients you know."

"I am really sorry about that. I never meant to steal Patricia away from you."

"It's alright just remember that you owe me one, that is the way it work's in your business and mine, we don't try and steal each other's clients but we live on referrals so if you know of anyone."

"Of course, if I hear of anyone I will contact you."

"Abby was one of David's client's at first."

"You're kidding."

"But he couldn't provide her with the kind of people she wanted. She prefers virgins or near virgins."

Marilyn was not that surprised. She was learning that there were so many people with a dark side a side full of lust that could be way beyond the normal that had to be satisfied. There was an awkward silence between them and then Marilyn could not stand it any longer so she reached out and pulled her close.

She found her chains and pulled on them gently, pushed up her blouse, and buried her face between her breasts and Leslie moaned as she kissed that favorite spot. She undid her jeans and found a string of pearls running between her cheeks and to the front.

"I was afraid that with your new job you wouldn't have time for me," Leslie said.

"I will always make time for you."

"And what will Madam Marilyn charge me."

"You will be my only free client."

"Thank you. There are vacancies in my building. I'm only ten minutes from downtown."

"I will think about it," Marilyn said and then she sucked on the pearls that ran between her legs.

David looked over Marilyn very carefully. She was wearing the battle gear. She had added a pair of black gloves that covered her arms past the elbow.

"Very nice, she looks really good, like Alvira. We may be able to sell that, Marilyn; mistress of the night."

Marilyn was buffed adding ten pounds of muscle to her arms, shoulders and legs.

"Where did those come from," David asked, pointing to her breasts that bulged out of the top of her corset.

"Tricks of the trade," Stephanie responded. She had used duct tape to sinche up and push every bit to the center of her chest and was working on a wire bra that would give the same look.

"Is she done training?"

"Soon," Stephanie said. "On Monday she will have her first client. I'm starting her with the White Whale."

"Good choice. I may have a special job for her later. Well, keep me posted."

"Who is the white whale?" Marilyn asked when he left.

"She is a white woman, very fat, one of the lowest paying clients. I'm sorry but you have to start at the bottom and work your way up to the better ones."

"I understand," Marilyn said as she removed her corset. It was like most sales and commission jobs you start out taking clients no one else wants. On her last job the first two accounts she worked for almost nothing just for the referrals but she was confident that if she honed her craft it would not be long before she could demand top dollar. Marilyn slowly started to peel off the duck tape.

"Let me help you," Stephanie said and then she squirted hand lotion on the tape.

"You won't have to wear that again. That was just to impress David."

"Was he serious about that Mistress of the dark thing?"

"Probable, he's always looking for something new, always looking for an angle. If it was legal he would have your picture on every bus in town. When I first started he had me dress up like little bo-peep for a couple of clients. He even got a sheep. The costume is around here somewhere."

Marilyn couldn't help but laugh even though the duct tape was almost taking her skin off.

"Well, if you had any hair there, you don't know," Stephanie said.

Marilyn took off the rest of the gear and put on a pair of shorts and a loose top.

"He started out as a mime in Central Park. He worked off Broadway for awhile, went out to Hollywood for awhile but couldn't make it as an actor so he was a male escort and made enough to come back here and buy a Triple X Theater. When porn went to video tape, he started this business."

It was like any other business Marilyn thought you have to change with the times; you adapt or go out of business.

"Did you and he ever?"

"Oh, heavens no I'm old enough to be his mother besides I believe he prefers young boys, just barely legal boys. Rule number sixteen in case you haven't been keeping track. Never, never, get romantically involved with a client and never get involved with the other staff, and stay off the booze and drugs and don't get hooked on pills so you are taking one to get through your day and another to bring you down at night. Try to treat it like any other job and don't let it consume you."

"Now come with me," Stephanie commanded. She was still dressed in her work clothes. She grabbed the whip and led her down a hallway and into one of the rooms.

She sat in a large chair on a raised platform and draped her legs over the arms, exposing her shaved, private area.

"Notice anything special about this room."

Marilyn had no clue what she was talking about all she could see were all the different restraints hanging from steel rods.

"There are no clocks. You don't want the client to think they are on a clock. You want them to think it's about pleasing them no matter long it takes. Try not to give them more than an hour of your time. Too little and they will feel cheated but you don't want it to drag on. After awhile you can tell when it's been about an hour. Now stand right there, no, over a little more."

In one quick motion she snapped the whip and Marilyn thought it came really close to hitting her.

"Now strip."

She snapped the whip again and Marilyn flinched.

"Didn't you hear me, I said strip."

Marilyn pulled off her top with trembling hands. She pulled down her shorts and stepped out of them. Stephanie jump down and grabbed her wrist, Marilyn resisted.

"They will resist too but they will give in because they want to be shackled."

She bound both writs with leather restraints.

"Is this part of the training?"

"Perhaps, or may be I just want to have my way with you. Not knowing what's going to happen next is what really gets them off. Never use the same routine twice, you can do the same thing but do it in a different order. You don't want it to become boring for them."

Stephanie ran her fingers between her cheeks and then massaged her ass. "What a beautiful ass."

She grabbed a riding crop off the wall and snapped it across her lower back, and then she grabbed her face.

"I want you to feel what they feel. Make sure all their weight is on their feet; make sure there is no pressure on their wrists. Marilyn had heard all this before in the other training sessions but now she was helpless, not knowing what was coming. She was excited and a little scared.

Stephanie brought the crop down hard across her ass and tears ran down Marilyn's cheeks from the pain. Then she ran her tongue up and down between her cheeks and kissed and bit at the tender flesh. Marilyn was moaning. She stood up, pulled her in close, letting the corset dig into her back.

"Yes, I could suck on your ass for hours but you have to stay detached, don't get too much into it. It will be like a fantasy for them but not for you."

Stephanie came around in front and pushed the riding crop between her legs. Marilyn had no choice but to spread her legs.

"You still need to shave down there. Would you like me to do it?"

"Yes, yes, I would."

She sucked on her engorged nipple, found her spot and worked it with one finger then two. Marilyn was shaking was getting very close and then she stopped.

"Bring them just to brink and then back off, especially the men. Do as many times as possible and when they finally come they will think they died and went to heaven."

She brought her to the brink two more times and Marilyn realized the power that she possessed; the power she would have, and then she had to ask, "Please?"

"Please, what?"

"Please get me off."

She worked her spot and then slipped two fingers inside and Marilyn exploded.

"You are really good."

"Thank you. There is one more thing you have to experience."

She got a long thin vibrator and put lubricant on it. She went around and ran it up and down between her cheeks and pressed the tip up against her opening.

"Be gentle here until you know what they can take or if they want it at all. Some will tell you, some can only moan, but use a steady, easy, push.

"Ram it in."

"You like it back here."

"Yes."

"Do like a dildo or a man back here."

"Both."

She worked it in slowly and then when the lubricant took hold she worked it in and out faster. She pushed it all the way in and turned the vibration to maximum then whipped her lightly with the ridding crop until Marilyn was begging and pleading for her never to stop.

"That was the best lesson of all."

"I thought you would like it," Stephanie said as she applied the shaving cream.

"Maybe I can return the favor sometime."

"Maybe."

Marilyn was still trying to get used to having weekends off. Even having Sunday off seemed strange and she was trying hard not to get nervous about her first client tomorrow. Her cell phone rang and she was hoping it was Leslie but knew from the caller Id that it was her mother. She figured that she had put her off long enough and it was now time for the inquisition so she agreed to have lunch with her at the country club. She picked out a long, flowered dress and as she put it on she wondered what her mother would think is she seen her in her work outfit. Would she be shocked, appalled, disgusted? For her mother, sex was something you did to have children. Sex wasn't supposed to be pleasurable. She was just to head out the door when she realized that all her make up was still on. She slicked down her hair and wiped all the makeup off. When she looked in the mirror she didn't like her image.

On the thirty minute train ride and fifteen minute cab ride to country club she had time to think about how she had not even thought about getting a man since she met Leslie. Did that mean she had really turned into a lesbian but she still didn't know what their relationship was, were they friends, lovers, or occasional lovers? And what was their future together? All she knew right then was that she was going to do what made her happy and Leslie made her happy.

She never liked the country club. Old money people complaining about the new money people and the dress code, dresses for women, and shirt and ties for men. And as the matridie escorted her to her mother's table she couldn't help but wonder if anyone at the club was one of their clients. It was certainly possible.

"What have you done," her mother said as soon as she sat down.

"What do you mean, mother."

"You look all, you know, pumped up."

Now Marilyn realized that she should have worn a business suite. The sun dress showed off too much of her shoulders and arms.

"I've had some free time so I've been working out. I am eating better. I feel great."

"I do admit you look healthier. You were always so pale and you had those awful bags under your eyes. Just don't turn into one of those women body builders, they are disgusting."

"No, I won't mother." But looking at those kind of woman had always excited Marilyn.

"Now tell me all about this new job."

"I can't mother, every thing I do is highly confidential." Deep down she hated not being able to be honest but her mother was not ready for the truth; she wasn't ready to tell her the truth. Besides she really did not know how long she would be doing it would she really like it once she started doing it every day. There were still so many unanswered questions.

"I get the feeling you are trying to hid something. Surely you can tell me something."

"It's just business."

"Is anyone from the club a client?"

"I don't think so."

"Surely you can at least give me one name."

It was the inquisition. What would her father of thought? Marilyn did not even want to think about that now or ever.

"Well, there is Patricia Long. You know her from college."

"Is that all?" Marilyn could tell she was not impressed. Thankfully the waiter came over to take their orders. There was time to regroup.

"If that is all the clients you have then I really am worried."

"Then there is Abby McKenzie."

"You mean from Desire, that Abby McKenzie?"

"Yes, mother." It was a lie but a small one because she was actually hoping she would be a client.

"Well that sounds better."

"There will be others."

"I just worry about your future. I know your father pushed you hard and I'm sure it wasn't easy getting both a law and business degree but he just wanted what was best for you. That's all any parent wants is what is best for their children and speaking of children."

"No, mother I'm not planning on any children."

"Tick tock, tick tock, dear. You are not getting any younger. I just don't understand your generation not wanting to settle down and have a family."

You never understood because you are petie, attractive, and elegant and not a brainy, stick woman, Marilyn thought. You had men drooling all over you when you were younger and I'm lucky that I got a date to the prom.

"I'm happy isn't that the most important thing."

"Security is important too. You've always sold yourself short. Any man would be lucky to have you as a wife."

They just don't want to go to bed with me or satisfy me, she thought. She wanted to scream out, have you ever been sexually satisfied? That's what is important for me and I don't care if it's by a woman.

"I had the pick of the litter when I was younger. I chose your father because he was stable and he was doing something important, protecting this country. Not like some of the cads in this place who made their money in banking or real estate. He made it to Admiral, that is very impressive and he was so handsome in his uniform. Speaking of families you haven't called your sister in weeks."

"I know, as soon as I get into a routine I will."

Mercifully the food finally arrived. She droned on about people at club and the gossip that she was not the least bit interested in but anything was better than talking about herself.

And on the way home she didn't want to think about it but deep down she knew that she had to. Her father would be ashamed of what she was doing. Giving people pleasure for pay wasn't honorable but weren't their whole other industries that gave people pleasure for money, bars, movies, the stage, sports but this was sexual pleasure so that made it bad and wrong. But he did tell her once that any work is good as long as it is honest. What she was doing was honest because there was no deceit, no trickery, no scamming. You pleased people and they paid you nothing is more honest than that and if don't please them you don't get paid. She wasn't going to rationize it any more, there was no one to impress anymore that burden had been lifted. She was just going to do it.

IXX

Marilyn was trying to control her breathing, trying not to get excited. Stephanie came over and massaged her shoulders.

"Are you nervous?"

"A little."

"You'll be fine."

"I probable should have asked before but does your family know what you do?"

"Sure."

"They don't mind?"

"Are you kidding, my family doesn't give a hoot. As long as I send money to my mother every month she's happy. My brother is a used car salesmen after two stints in the joint. My sister has three kids by three different guys and lives on welfare. But I bet your family is different. If you are having second thoughts maybe you shouldn't be going in there."

"I'm not. I just wonder if they would ever accept it."

"I don't know. I can't imagine that they would cast you out and call you the devil child. But you never know maybe some day you will have to choose. I wouldn't worry about that right now you are just getting started besides you're not married to this job. Are you ready?"

"Yes, I'm ready."

Marilyn slipped into the room though a hidden door and climbed into the chair. The room was totally dark except for two small spot lights that illuminated a heavy, middle aged woman. Marilyn hit a switch on the chair and it was illuminated by a spot light.

"Where is Stephanie?"

"Silence," Marilyn said and then she cracked the whip. The backlash almost caught her arm.

"She is indisposed, now strip."

"I don't know I'm used to Stephanie."

Marilyn stood up and cracked the whip. "Didn't you hear me, I said strip."

The woman reached back and unzipped her dress. Her hands and arms were trembling.

Marilyn just stood there with her hands on her hips trying to show strength and power.

"The longer you make me wait the more severe the beating will be."

She took off her bra and her huge breasts cascaded down and rested on her stomach. Her rolls of fat completely hid her panties. She pulled them down and then Marilyn came down off the platform and grabbed her face, licked it, and then sucked on her ear. Then she whispered into her ear, "I'm Madame Marilyn and if don't like me you don't have to pay but I'm going to have my way with you whether you pay or not because I want to."

Marilyn went in back of her reached around and grabbed her huge breasts.

"You really have some big tits. I like big tits." She massaged them until she was moaning. She was planning to shackle her writs but then she remerred what Stephanie had said about doing the unexpected and that was probable something she was used to so Marilyn grabbed the riding crop and used it to pick up one of her breasts. Marilyn could not believe it was taking all her strength just to lift one of them.

"I don't whether I want to beat you or have my way with you or both."

Marilyn got down on her knees and sucked on one of the massive breasts, massaged the other one and put her hand between her legs. She was really getting into sucking on her nipple when she realized that she was not listening to her breathing so she listened and Marilyn figured she was close and it was too soon. She massaged her tits roughly.

"What a big set of tits."

Marilyn walked around inspecting her trying to remain detached and remembering what Stephanie had said about developing her own style and giving the client something new and she figured that she was probable used to be beating and humiliated so maybe it was time for something different. Marilyn pulled her close and dug her corset into her back.

"I've decided I'm going have my way with you."

"Why would you want me you are so beautiful and I'm so fat and disgusting?" Marilyn could feel her whole body shake with excitement.

"I love to doing big fat women until they scream and I'm going to make you really scream. Now get on the platform on your knees." Marilyn never saw a big woman move that fast. She figured the platform would put at the right height and it did. Marilyn slipped on a pair of latex panties with an attached dildo. She ran her fingers between her cheeks and then her whole fist.

"What a big ass, I love big asses." Marilyn tried to massage it like it was the greatest thing in the world. She put her hand between her legs and it was like a lake. It was too late she had already had an orgasm. Marilyn knew they had more time and she should have controlled her more but figured another orgasm or two wouldn't hurt besides this was her first. The dildo slipped in and Marilyn worked it in and out adding more force with every inward thrust so in a few minutes white whale was panting, sweating, and grunting all at the same time.

"Now scream for me baby," she said as she dug her finger nails into her breasts. She did scream and the orgasm took her breath away. Marilyn sucked on her ear and massaged her tits.

"Thank you I needed that," she said after catching her breath.

Marilyn whispered in her ear, "What you need honey is to find a man who likes big fat women but then I would miss our fun together."

Marilyn sat in the chair with her legs over the arms exposing everything.

"Now get up here and service me."

She wasted no time in sticking her tongue deep inside. Marilyn ran the handle of the riding crop up and down her back.

"You can please yourself while you do me." Marilyn watched her hand disappear between her legs and then she whipped her back lightly with the riding crop until that big body shook again and hers shook a little.

Marilyn came in the dressing room and grabbed a towel.

"How long was it?"

"Sixty eight minutes very good for your first time," Stephanie replied

"I can't believe how exciting that was."

"But was it exciting for the client."

Now Marilyn wondered if it really was that exciting for her or did she spend too much time worrying about or own needs. Jimmy came barging in like he always did even when they were stark naked. Marilyn figured he was a totally gay or really got off thinking about them when he got home.

"Stephanie, housewife, in number four. A tip from white whale."

Marilyn held up a hundred dollar bill.

"Wow," Stephanie said, "I think you made an impression."

There was a whipping accident with the next client which resulted in a full refund and David was not pleased. The rest of the week went better as she was more focused but her own needs were unmet. Even Friday night was about Patricia's needs because she was paying. She needed Leslie. On Saturday she went to the building on the pretense of looking at one of the condos but she wasn't there so she looked at one of the units. She was impressed. They were not very large but plenty of room for just her. She sat in the lobby and ran some preliminary numbers on a calculator. With the sale of her house at even market value she could buy the condo and have profit of at least sixty thousand, maybe eighty. Marilyn erased the numbers from the memory and was just starting to reenter the numbers factoring in standard sales commissions and closing costs when she looked up and Leslie was standing there.

"So, did you look at a unit?"

"Yes, they are very nice. I think its very duable."

Marilyn was still wearing her make up from work, the shortest skirt and the tightest top she could find.

"Would you like to come up for coffee?"

"I would love to."

As Leslie filled the coffee pot Marilyn realized she really didn't know that much about her and that made her nervous. As far as she knew she could have a boyfriend and she was just using her for a quick thrill.

"Let's cut crap," Marilyn finally said. "I want you, I need you. I need you in my life."

Leslie came over and kissed her and then said, "You're so hot."

"Can I spend the night?"

Leslie unbuttoned her blouse and let it fall to the floor. "Do you still want me if I look like this?" Gone was the nipple rings, gone were the chains.

"Can we make love all night?" Marilyn said.

Leslie took her hand and led her into the bedroom and in a few minutes she had that passion between her legs that she craved. They enjoyed each other for hours and then talked for a couple of hours. Right before they went to sleep, they both agreed that Marilyn would be moving as soon as possible.

Marilyn liked the way Leslie looked in the morning but it was driving her little crazy since she was toasting bagels completely naked. She was just about to suggest something obscene when her cell phone rang in the other room. Marilyn went into the bedroom and started getting dressed and then Leslie came in.

"It's Stephanie and she is sick at work and has a client."

"On a Sunday?"

"I know, she said that she had things going on the side but I didn't think she was doing clients at work after hours."

"Not even time for breakfast."

"I will grab something at the station and have it on the train."

Leslie caught her by surprise, pushed her down on the bed, and then straddled her head.

"Then do me, do me fast." She did and Marilyn loved leaving with the taste and smell of her.

When she got to work, Stephanie was laying on the bed in the dressing room white as a ghost. Marilyn sat on the bed and put her hand on her forehead.

"You look terrible. Do you want me to call an ambulance?"

"I'll be alright. Just don't have a pizza with the works and tacos in the same sitting.

"Your pregnant you should be eating better than that."

"It was just one of those cravings you know." Marilyn had no idea and probable never would. "Dark helmet will be her anytime so you need to take care of him."

"Are you kidding, he's your client. I wouldn't know what to do. I will explain to him that you are sick and have him reschedule."

"It's very inconvient for him to come here and I don't want to disappoint him." He was not only Stephanie's best client he was the establishment's best client. His referrals had brought in many new clients.

"I take it David doesn't know about this."

"I told you that I had things on the side."

"But here. What if David finds out?"

"The hell with David without us he's got nothing. Now please get ready I don't want to disappoint him. Just remember he likes it rough and from behind." Stephanie jerked up and dashed to the bathroom.

Marilyn quickly got her make up on and the battle gear. He was already in the room when she went in so she quickly grabbed his wrist and restrained him with the leather cuffs.

"Where is Stephanie?"

"I'm sorry she is ill," she whispered into his ear. His entire head was covered by a leather helmet hiding his identity. She cuffed the other wrist.

"Is she alright?" Marilyn thought he sounded very concerned and wondered if he was the father but had no way of knowing and no way of asking.

"Just something she ate. She is very disappointed that she couldn't torture you herself but it looks like I get to have some fun."

She stood in front of him, hands on her hips. From the few gray hairs in the middle of his chest she figured he had to be middle age or older. She cracked the whip.

"Now let's get down to business." She cracked it again and she noticed that he was already getting hard and eyeing her breasts.

"You like these, honey. Then why don't you have a taste?" She bent his head down and buried his face between her breasts and then reached around and scraped her nails across his back. He sucked on her cleavage. She pulled down one of the cups and exposed her nipple.

"Why don't suck on this."

She reached down and grabbed his shaft barely getting her fingers around it. She moved her hand up and down and his breathing became erratic. Suddenly she choked off the bottom of his shaft like Stephanie had showed her.

"Oh, not yet baby. You haven't earned your please yet. I want you to beg for it. Do you understand me?" she asked and pulling up on his strodum.

"Yes, I understand."

She sucked on one of his nipples then the other and then back and forth from one to the other all time choking him off and then she applied the nipple clamps. She then whipped his ass several times with the riding crop trying to use a gental hand. She kissed him working her tongue into his mouth and pumped his shaft until he was close and then choked him off again.

"Oh, not yet baby," she said as she bit his lower lip.

"Please-"

She cut him off by grabbing his sack and squeezing.

"Please what?"

"Please do what ever you want?"

"That's what I thought."

She whipped him several more times and then put on the dildo and pushed between his cheeks. He lifted up his ass and moved backwards.

"Oh, baby likes this, maybe a little too much," so she pulled it away.

She got down on her knees, massaged his cheeks, sucked them, pushed them apart, and then used her tongue. He was moaning and grunting as she expertly used her tongue. She worked on him for a long time and then came around to the front and grabbed his shaft pumping up and down.

"Please, please," he begged.

"Please do my ass first."

"I don't know if you deserve it."

"Please, you can whip me first if you want." And she did just enough to sting but not enough to leave any marks. She lubricated the dildo and pushed it between his cheeks and then held it still. He moved around until the dildo was where he needed it and she pushed it in with a slow, steady, movement. She reached around and removed the nipple clamps and then worked each nipple between her finger and thumb. She massaged his sac and shaft until his ejaculation covered her hand and arm. She went and got a pan of warm soapy water and washed him and his moans signaled his approval. She then kissed him deeply as she lubricated his shaft and then she whispered into his ear "This is from Stephanie." She undid the wrist restraints and then turned around and spread her cheeks. As his thick shaft worked in and out she knew that she wasn't suppose to be enjoying it but she was. It was supposed to be all about his pleasure but she couldn't help it. His thickness and steady movement was intoxicating. She pleased herself until she felt him explode again.

After washing him again, Marilyn went in the dressing room and Stephanie was on the bed looking worse than before. Marilyn called 911, quickly changed her clothes, and after an argument over medical insurance with the EMT, rode in the ambulance to the county medical facility. Marilyn stayed until the doctor assured her that she would be fine but they were keeping her for observation. Marilyn went home, took a bath, and then Leslie massaged her feet and back. She was exhausted. She thought it would be awkward sleeping with Leslie but she liked the warmth and smell of her body next to her.

When she woke up Leslie came in to the bedroom and straddled her on the bed. She was wearing a leather harness. The leather straps ran down her back, over her shoulders and circled her breasts pushing them up and out.

"Sinch me up."

Marilyn undid the buckle and pulled up on the leather strap running between her legs.

"More. That's it. It's digging in real nice."

"Are you going to the hospital?"

"Yes."

"I am going to stay harnessed like this until you come back and release me."

Marilyn wanted her more than ever, more than anything.

When she walked into the small hospital room, crowded with three other patients the doctor was giving her his instructions. Stephanie looked much better. Her color had returned.

"I afraid at your age you may have a very difficult pregnancy. I'm not a specialist but you should really think about quit working or you run the risk of losing the baby."

"You should go see a specialist," Marilyn responded.

"By all means, if you can afford it," the doctor snapped back.

Marilyn knew what he meant. When she checked Stephanie in, she had put entertainment as her profession and she assumed the doctor thought they were hookers or call girls. Marilyn was still wearing all her makeup, wearing it more and more. It was becoming a part of her. I'm sure we make more per hour than you do, Marilyn thought.

"You can leave when you're ready."

"Thank you, doctor." Stephanie said.

The doctor gave Marilyn a look but she wasn't sure if he was looking down at her or he was interested.

"Are you sure, you are alright?"

"I'll be fine. The doctor is probable right. I can't be doing what I'm doing. I'm not twenty any more."

"You should do see a specialist."

"Where is my purse?"

She dumped most of it on the bed and then unzipped a compartment in the bottom of the bag and handed Marilyn a pass book savings. Marilyn opened it. The balance was hundred thousand and change.

"You know all about money management, right?"

"I know more about what not to do with your money."

Stephanie gave her a puzzled look.

"Yes, I have managed my own portfolio for years."

"Well, I want you to set up a trust or something for the baby. In case something happens to me. I will give you ten percent."

"I would be happy too but I couldn't take anything."

"Then I will find someone else," Stephanie said grabbing the book from her.

"Alright, I'll do it but I will charge you ten percent commission on the growth of your portfolio, over time it will be a much better deal for me."

"Never give it away for free," Stephanie said as she handed her back the pass book.

"Do you have life insurance?"

"No."

"Well the first thing is life insurance that gains cash value incase your daughter wants to do to college."

"That would be nice. You can handle all that." Stephanie said as she patted her hand. "You know Marge and Johnny want the same kind of help. I have already talked to them. Make sure you charge them a decent fee. They tried a couple of places but I guess no one really wanted to help them."

"I would be happy too." Marilyn wondered if it was because of what they did. She figured money was money but she had once been part of that uptown crowd who looked down on people like them.

David and Jimmy came bounding in.

"So how's my girl?" David asked.

"I'm fine."

"So are you ready to go back to work?"

"Your compassion is overwhelming." Marilyn snapped.

"I sent flowers. Didn't I tell you to send flowers?" David asked Jimmy.

"I'm sorry, I must have forgotten."

They all knew he was too cheap.

"Seriously, I have a business to run. You will be back to work, right?"

"I don't thing so David," Stephanie responded

"That's not good."

"Marilyn can easily take over."

"Jimmy, what's our status?"

"With just one of you that would mean three clients a day, seven days a week."

"How can that be, David?"

"He went out and got more clients," Marilyn responded.

"Well, there was two of your working."

"Marilyn was supposed to be my replacement."

"That is just great David," Marilyn said. "Well, you better find me some help or I'm walking."

David was dumbfounded.

"I'm serious David. You either get me some help or I'm walking."

"Alright, I will. I promise."

Stephanie was looking for something to throw at him.

"Good by David." Marilyn quipped.

"Come on Jimmy, I know when I'm out gunned."

"Get well," Jimmy said. "We miss you."

"Can you believe that guy?" Stephanie said.

A few moments later a nurse brought in a huge bouquet of flowers.

"Not from David?" Stephanie asked.

There was a large card attached. Marilyn handed it to Stephanie and then watched the nurse leave.

"Stop that," Stephanie said.

"Stop what?"

"Stop mentally undressing her."

"I wasn't."

"I can't believe it." Stephanie said. Marilyn looked at her and tears were whelling up in her eyes. She handed Marilyn the card. She opened it. It was a normal get well card with the initials DH on the inside but there was a check inside. Marilyn opened it. It was for ten thousand dollars.

"Who is this guy?" Marilyn asked.

"It's best if you never find out."

When Marilyn got home, Leslie was at the kitchen table in a bathrobe that was loosely tied at the waist and parted showing all of her leg.

"How is Stephanie?"

"Fine, but she won't be able to work anymore." Marilyn said as she sat down. "And David went out and got more clients thinking that we both would be working."

"So, you are going to very busy."

"It looks like it."

"Well, then we better take advantage of your time off." Leslie stood up, untied the robe and it fell to the floor. Marilyn stared at how the leather harness pushed up her breasts making them stick out, crying for attention. Marilyn grabbed the straps that ran down her stomach and pulled her in close. She sucked on each breast and then each nipple.

"You taste so good."

She reached between her legs finding the leather strap was all wet. Leslie turned around and bent over showing her how the strap went between her cheeks.

"I want you to suck that right out of there."

And she did and then she sucked on the part that went between her legs and she like the taste and smell of leather and her juice. Then she whipped her until she was begging to be taken and Marilyn took her hard and fast. Leslie then crawled between her legs and stayed there for over two hours and every time Marilyn begged her to stop because she couldn't possible have another orgasm she proved her wrong.

In a couple of weeks, Marilyn was working harder than she ever did on her old job. Servicing all the clients, setting up and implementing portfolios for Stephanie, Mary and Johnny at work, plus drawing up plans to start her own business had her going night and day. Leslie helped as much as she could. Just having her at the end of the day was a great comfort for Marilyn. Finally she had to hire a financial planner because it was taking up too much of her time. She hired a designing firm to make a restraing rack that could fit into a large suite case on wheels. It took all of the time management skills she had learned on in college and on her previous job to balance all the demands for her time. White whale was demanding more and more visits, DH was now a regular but her favorite new client was just referred to as Uptown Lady not only because she was seeing her on the side but because it was quick and there was always an envelope with five one hundred dollar bills inside. She would just lift up her skirt, pull down her panties and Marilyn would quickly enter her and just pump in and out until she held up her hand letting her know that was enough. There was never any talking, or fore play, just hurry up and get it done. They did it once in her limo and once it a freight elevator. The instructions on how and where to meet her was always delivered by messenger. They were always very precise and when she got to the destination she was always wearing a plastic mask the kind a burgler would use. She didn't know if it was to hide her identity or a deformity because there was scaring on the back of her hands and neck. This day the instructions took her uptown, down two alleys and through a service entrance. She took the service elevator per the instructions to the fortieth floor. In her long, black, trench coat Marilyn felt like a spy or a secret agent. She went down a service hallway and through a door where she found herself in a large office. The woman was talking on the phone, her mask was on, and she was wearing a dark business suite. She motioned Marilyn over as she continued to talk on the phone and then she lifted up her skirt and pulled down her panties while all the time talking on the phone. Marilyn got behind her and as she took of her trench coat and adjusted the strap-on dildo, she looked out the window and saw her old office building. She motioned to begin so Marilyn pushed in slowly and worked it in and out very slowly. From the one-sided conversation Marilyn could tell they were talking about estate planning. She hung up the phone, used the desk for leverage, and pushed herself down hard on the dildo. She was breathing hard when she held up her hand and Marilyn thought she was done because it usually only lasted about ten minutes but she took off her suite coat when Marilyn pulled out the dildo.

"More," was all she said.

Marilyn pumped in and out harder than before and looked at the scaring on her arms that was exposed by her short, sleeved blouse. Marilyn in one quick motion undid her bra from the back, reached around and pushed up the cups and started massaging her small breasts through the blouse. She was transfixed. Marilyn then slid her hand underneight her blouse and felt the scarring up her stomach and to her nipples.

"No don't"

"Shhhh," Marilyn replied.

Marilyn started to unbutton her blouse."

"You don't have too."

"I want too."

Marilyn unzipped her corset so their skin could touch. She stood motionless as Marilyn massaged her breasts. She massaged them for a long time until she said, "Can, I lay on top of you naked. I will pay you extra."

"You don't have pay extra," Marilyn replied

They both got totally naked, Marilyn got down on the floor, and she got on top inserting the dildo inside of her. Marilyn massaged her scared back and her smooth ass. Marilyn slid the mask off very slowly. The skin of her face was taught and the eyes were out of shape. Marilyn kissed her gently and then more forcefully and she could feel her tears. When Marilyn left if there was any shame in what she was doing, deep down inside, it was now gone.

XX

When Leslie came in the kitchen, Marilyn said, "I wish you wouldn't dress like that." She was wearing nothing but a short wrap that barely covered her ass.

"Like what?"

She turned around letting the wrap come open in the front exposing her clamps and chains.

"You know it drives me crazy. And I don't have time right now. I have to meet DH in a little while."

Leslie came over and massaged her back.

"Sorry baby. Are you working on your business plan?"

"Yes, I have five good clients right now. I plan to give them each a color coded walkie talkie. They each have a different frequency so I will know who will be calling me. I just don't know how I am going to service them all when they want it because it's a twenty minute train ride into the city then I have to take a cab."

Leslie massaged her back and neck. "You can't be on-call twenty four seven that would be crazy. Just tell them they have to be either day or night time clients. You could hire a car and driver."

"You mean a big limo."

"No, just a small town car, something big enough you can change in. You could hire a driver with some protection experience. You do carry around large sums of cash. I worry about that. Besides you said that you have been hassled on the train."

"That is a great idea. Some of the men think I'm a hooker like I'm going to service them on the train."

The door bell rang. "I better get that," Marilyn said. "I don't think you're dressed for it."

"It all depends on who it is," Leslie responded.

Marilyn wheeled in a very large suitcase.

"What's that?" Leslie asked.

"You'll find out later. I have to run."

"I hope it's wicked."

"It will be."

Marilyn waited an extra hour but DH was a no show. She took a cab to the train station and just missed a train. Leslie was right, Marilyn thought. I have to get a car.

She went into the lunch room and took a seat at the counter.

A man came and sat next to her. He was wearing a large black overcoat and a fordora pulled down so the brim was over his eyes.

"You are being followed Miss Winters."

She looked at him closely but he was unfamiliar but the voice was familiar. He slid a picture over to her. It was picture of man in a car with a camera. He was parked down the alley way from the client entrance.

"Who is he?"

"A private detective."

"Why is a detective following me?"

"I suggest you ask your mother."

"Are you DH."

"We can have no more contact Miss Winters."

"No, please wait," Marilyn said as she grabbed his arm.

"Listen I will meet you, I mean him anywhere at anytime. Here," she said as she pulled out one of the walkie talkies she had been trying out. "He can contact me with this. I'm the only one who has the other one."

He took it from her. "He may be in touch."

Marilyn was furious by the time the train arrived. She immediately called her mother on her cell phone and told her in no uncertain terms what she thought about envading her privacy. By the time she got home she was thinking that was probable not the smartest way to handle the situation.

"What wrong," Leslie asked as soon as she got in the door.

"Nothing, I can't handle."

Marilyn pulled the suitcase out into the living room.

"Time me," Marilyn said.

Marilyn unsnapped the hard cover of the suite case, put the wheels down flat, and then pulled them out. She lifted out the counter weights that were attached to small pipes and pushed them into two of the wheels, pulled out the telescoping, aluminum poles and attached them to the other two wheels then attached the cross bar. She pulled down on the cross bar as hard as she could and it did not bend or tip.

"How long?"

"Less than five minutes."

"Good, that will be good." Marilyn grabbed Leslie by the hand. The cross bar was too high so she adjusted it. She would mark it later with a color pen, a different color for each person. She took out the wrist restraints. The whip was in there and even a telescoping riding crop. In the lid were numerous dildos and strap on devices. Marilyn brought down the riding crop hard on her ass liked the way it made her ass shake and quiver.

"Please don't beat me."

Marilyn reached around and massaged her tits and pulled on her chains.

"I don't know what I want to do, beat you, have you, or both."

"Please don't beat me and rape me."

Marilyn beat her and then used every device in the suite case and couldn't believe how much she enjoyed it. Maybe she was taking out her frustrations from her mother's hiring someone to spy on her. She felt bad later about the marks on her ass but knew Leslie loved it because she went right to sleep right after a powerful orgasm. Marilyn was laying there awake listening to Leslie's gentle breathing and feeling drained. This job was both physical and mental. I have to start scheduling some days off, she thought. It felt like she had just gotten to sleep when she heard the door buzzer. She looked through the key hole and it was a messenger. She took the envelope and ripped it open. Inside were ten one hundred dollar bills and instructions. She really wanted the day off but it was a client being referred by dark helmet. Leslie was still asleep when she left. She was wondering if it was wise to write I love you on the note she left for Leslie as she rode the train into the city.

It took almost two hours to find the necessary props and to arrive at the address. The cab drove up a circle drive and stopped in front of a mansion. It was very stately looking the kind you would see in magazines or an old civil war movie. She gave the cabbie a big tip and told him to return in two hours. She checked her outfit, a plain black, dress that came way below the knees. It buttoned down the front. A straight black wig came just below her ears, no nylons, just platform shoes with a three inch heals, black lipstick, no other makeup, and round glasses. She had a small shoulder bag and a clipboard. She rang the door bell and in a few moments the door opened very slowly.

"I'm from the agency," Marilyn said.

"Yes ma'am, please come in," said a maid.

She was shorter even than Leslie, very cute, and was wearing a French maid outfit. Marilyn was surprised that anyone really wore those things anymore. The foyer was huge. There was a chandelier hanging in the middle of the room with a winding staircase and paintings on the wall.

"Please follow me to the study."

Again, just like a movie, it was lined with books, a large oak desk in the center, big leather couch to one side.

"I'm here for the inspection."

"Yes, ma'am."

"Should I begin?"

"Yes, ma'am."

Marilyn pulled out a white glove out of her purse and put it on. She walked around the room running a finger over the desk and book cases pretending to check things off on the clipboard. She avoided touching the vases and statues near the windows figuring they cost more than she could make in a year. She lifted up an ashtray that was on a small table.

"Come over here," Marilyn commanded.

The maid came over and she pointed at the table.

"You should be able to see your face in this table. It should shine. I'm very disappointed."

"I'm very sorry ma'am."

"That's not good enough; you know what you have to do."

"Yes ma'am."

She ran quickly and got some polish and started working on the table. Marilyn sat in one of the big leather chairs, thankful to be off her feet for a few minutes. The maid quickly did the desk. Marilyn pretended to write on the clipboard and then said, "On to the kitchen." After a tour around the kitchen, Marilyn said, "I don't think I've ever see such a pig sty. It is just deplorable."

"I try and do my best ma'am."

"Well it is totally unacceptable. You know what you have to do."

The maid went over and bent over the table.

"The panties too," Marilyn barked.

She pulled down her panties and then Marilyn used the clipboard ten times hard on her bare ass.

"Now the bedrooms."

After each inspection of a bedroom there was another spanking with the clipboard. When Marilyn thought enough time had gone by she said, "Your work here is totally unacceptable. I don't see there is any choice but to let you go."

"Oh, no, please ma'am I will do anything. Please don't let me go."

"Anything."

"Yes, anything."

Marilyn reached down and unbuttoned the last four buttons of her dress. She sat on the bed and spread her legs.

"Now you will come over here and service me. Have you ever done a woman before?"

"No ma'am, never."

"Well you better do it better than you clean or you will be out of job."

"I will do my best."

Marilyn tried to stay detached but her mouth and tongue were like precision tools. She found herself grabbing fistfuls of the bed cover with both hands and hanging on for dear life, trying not to scream out in pure pleasure. Finally she couldn't hold back any longer and gasped when she exploded spaying juice all over her face.

"Do I please you, ma'am."

"No," Marilyn responded out of breath. "So you know what you have to do."

As she stood up there was no doubt what was making her panties stick out in front. I can't believe it, Marilyn thought, this cute, little, thing with a mouth and tongue from heaven is a guy. She spanked him ten more times.

"Can I have another chance to please you ma'am."

"This is your last chance."

It took all of Marilyn's will power not to lie down and let that wonderful mouth and tongue do her forever. After another explosion she pushed him away.

"I think you have saved your job for now," Marilyn said and then stood up and buttoned her dress. Her inner thighs were wet down to her knees and her legs were weak.

"Thank you, ma'am. I will try and do better next time." Heaven help me if you can, Marilyn thought.

"I sure hope you can if you want to keep this job."

All Marilyn could thing about on the cab ride to the train station was I should be paying him and she still had a fill days work ahead of her.

There was a steady hand on the buzzer and it was driving Jimmy crazy. He was running from room to room picking up money trying not to look at the clients getting dressed, escorting new clients to the changing rooms. Finally he made it to the front entrance and looked at the security monitor. It was a woman he had never seen before.

"Can I help you?"

Finally, she released the buzzer.

"I'm here to see Marilyn."

"She is with a client. Don't you have a key?"

"No, I don't have a key. I'm her mother."

Jimmy didn't know what to do. Tell her to go away, go tell Marilyn, call David, or tell her to go away.

"I'm sorry she is with a client."

"I'm going to keep ringing the buzzer until you let me in." and she did. Jimmy hit the door switch and then went to the entrance.

"Like I said, she is with a client and it may be awhile."

"You go tell her I'm here, young man. I will wait here until she is done." Jimmy had no doubt from the tone of her voice that she

S.L. Hendrickson

would stand there until hell froze over. He had never interrupted a session before.

"Come with me."

He took her to the dressing room. On the way there they met Jason in the hallway and he was wearing nothing but a thong. She averted her eyes.

"You can wait for her in here."

She walked around the room looking at the different restraints and costumes. She picked up a leopard print bra and thong holding it like it may be contaminated.

Pricilla came in wearing a nurse's uniform.

"Clients are not allowed back here."

"I'm not a client of this place, young lady," she said sternly. "I'm Marilyn's mother."

"I see. I'm sure she will be done soon."

She took off the nurse's uniform. She was now totally nude except for white nylons and a pair of black high heels. Martha averted her eyes for a few moments then stared at her enormous breasts. Pricilla grabbed some wet wipes and removed her make up. In a few moments she went from a nurse to French aristocrat including a huge blond wig and jewelry. The jewelry went around her neck and fell between her massive cleavage. She was half way to the door when she stopped and said, "Damn, there are no nylons or high heels in the 17th century." She removed them and hustled out the door in bare feet.

She looked at more of the costumes and groaned when she held a waitress uniform to herself and it barely came down below her waist.

Marilyn came in drying herself with a towel. White whale had given her a real work out and she was debating if she wanted her as a client when she left so she didn't even notice her mother in the room as she sat down on a chair and stated wiping down her inner thighs.

"So, this is what you do for a living. I don't know what to think Marilyn. You have sex with perverts for money."

"I give people sexual pleasure and I like it."

"For gods sake Marilyn you are a Harvard graduate."

"For once in my life I'm happy, isn't that important."

"You're father would be ashamed."

120

"Don't throw father at me, he is long gone and I can't please him now and I doubt that I ever could."

Marilyn finally realized she was exposing herself so she turned around in the chair and at that moment didn't like what she saw in the mirror.

"He just wanted you to be happy."

"No, he just wanted to control me like one of his soldiers."

"That is unfair."

"No, what was unfair is that you never spent anytime making me feel attractive like you did with Barb. Now I feel wanted and needed, even attractive and desirable, and I like it."

"We can get you help Marilyn, a good psychiatrist."

"Have you ever had sexual pleasure, mother? I didn't think so. So until you do maybe you should be the one going to the psychiatrist."

There was silence now. It had all been said. The line between them had been drawn.

"If you come to your senses you know where I will be and go see your sister."

Marilyn handed the walkie talkie to the driver. "Buzz me exactly at seven. I will tell you if I'm ready to leave."

"Yes, ma'am."

"It shouldn't be past eight either way."

She walked up to the modest three bedroom house. There was no white picket fence but it was located in one of the prime suburbs. The makeup was gone. She looked like she had a lifetime ago, plane, dressed in a business suite. Marilyn and Barb hugged.

"Who was that," her husband Ken said as the car pull away.

"It's just my driver."

"You have a car and a driver?" Ken said raising his eyebrows.

Ken and Marilyn shook hands.

"Where are the kids?" Marilyn asked.

"They are down the street, one of their kids just a new video so they begged to go see it and have pizza." Marilyn figured it was an excuse and now she felt like a leper.

"You look good," Ken said. "Would you like a drink?"

"Lemon, water would be fine." Marilyn noticed he was checking her out. She wondered if he was mentally undressing her, was he seeing her as a desirable woman or a freak?

"Did you remodel?"

"We just painted and got new carpet," Ken responded.

That was it Marilyn thought, nothing left to talk about. Ken was a network systems engineer and Barb was the stay at home Mom. They were worlds apart.

"How's business?" Ken asked and immediately his face turned red.

Marilyn decided quickly that she wasn't going to hide anything. "Business is very good. My client list is growing all the time. I should be able to be working for myself by the end of the month. My best friend at work is six months pregnant and having her first child at age fifty two. She is having a difficult pregnancy. Leslie just got her PhD in sexual therapy and is planning on opening her own clinic very soon. I finally sold that terrible house. I am managing the portfolios of three people at work. I keep busy."

"I see," Barb said. Her world was full of PTA meetings, soccer practices, and school bazaars.

"Did you really tell your mother where to go?" Ken asked as he handed her the drink.

"Please, Ken," Barb responded.

"Well, if you did, you have more guts than I do. She has been meddling in our lives since we got married. According to her I should be vice president by now. I like what I'm doing. What's wrong with that?"

"No argument from me," responded Marilyn.

"I believe dinner is ready." Barb said.

Through dinner Marilyn heard about each of the kids and their teachers, their neighbor's idocanstrise but it seemed too unreal for Marilyn. There was a lack of immediacy that existed in her world. They were in two different worlds she was now like one of the night people who came out only after the so called normal people went home to their so called normal lives.

"Well, I will let you girls gab," Ken said. Marilyn heard the television come on.

"Of course mother told be about the private detective," Barb said as she started to clear the table.

"Did she tell you that it may have cost us our best client?"

"No, I'm still not sure what you do, Mother was a little vague. She just said you were working with perverts."

Marilyn looked her straight in the eye. "I give sexual satisfaction to men and women for money."

Barb put away some things and rinsed off a few things. She sat down at the table.

"Ken is a good provider and he is great with the kids but he has never really done it for me if you know what I mean. He is the only man I've ever been with."

Marilyn could not believe what she was hearing. She wanted to scream to the heavens, I can't believe that you have had three kids and never had an orgasm. Marilyn got her purse and got out an Avalon card and handed it to her.

"I don't need therapy or anything, I just want to."

"You just want to experience it."

"Yes, what about where you work?"

"Trust me this will be much better and don't worry about the cost. I will take care of it. When you call just give them my name."

"Thank you." Marilyn couldn't help but feel some sense of vindication.

Her walkei talkie buzzed and she took it out of her purse and hit it twice giving the signal for eight.

"Do you have to go?"

"Not yet."

The kids came in. The youngest Brian, age five, ran into the kitchen and stopped dead in his tracks.

"We saw a movie."

"What kind of movie?" Marilyn asked.

"I don't know, a blue thing, with big ears."

"It was a cartoon," Gabriel said from the door way. She was the oldest, twelve going on sixteen.

"What did you bring us," Brian asked.

"Brian, she doesn't have to bring you anything," Barb scolded.

"I don't know did I bring you anything?" Marilyn responded. She went through her purse and through the pockets of her suite coat and pulled out a miniature Statue of Liberty. "See, when you push here the torch lights up and it glows in the dark."

He grabbed it made the torch light up and then ran off with it.

"You sure are an attractive young lady," Marilyn said to Gabriel. She had her grandmother features.

In a couple moments Ken Junior came into the kitchen.

"Looking for presents?" Marilyn asked.

"These kids are terrible." Barb responded.

Marilyn took a game out of her purse and handed it to him.

"No way, Sports 3000, these won't be out for months?"

"I know people."

"Thank you, Aunt Marilyn."

Gabriel came over and put her arms around Marilyn.

"Did I forget you?" Maybe I did."

Gabriel sat on her lap like a little girl. Marilyn reached into the other inside pocket and pulled out an executive electronic organizer that could also be used to download music.

"You're kidding, for me."

"Now that's way too much, Marilyn." Barb said.

"How often do I get to come spoil them?"

"You can come anytime Barb said and her too."

"You mean Leslie."

"Yes."

"Will you come in my room and show me how to use it, please,"

In her room, were pictures of young men, some with their shirts off and Marilyn had no idea who they were. The only pictures her mother would let her put up were pictures of horses.

Marilyn sat on the bed and took the organizer out of its case.

"Grandma says your evil because you sell your body to men for money."

Marilyn was shocked that she would even talk to her about it let alone call her evil.

"Do you have intercourse with men?"

"You know about that."

"Of course, we learned about it in school. I know all about intercourse, lesbians, gays, and getting pregnant."

"I didn't know anything at your age. I satisfy men but we don't have intercourse."

"Do you use masturbation?"

"Yes, do you think about that sometimes."

"Yes."

"Well it's very natural and there is nothing wrong with it and don't let anyone tell you different now lets concentrate on this."

XXI

The driver was weaving in and out of the heavy noon hour traffic. Marilyn kept looking at her watch. She was going to be late for Uptown woman. The schedule was getting to her, working for David, taking care of her own clients and just then her cell phone rang and one of the walkie talkies buzzed at the same time.

"Damn," she said as she grabbed the cell phone.

"Stephanie, can you please hold."

She opened up the small case that carried the now six walkie talkies.

"Meet me tomorrow at the Kingston Hotel, at 6 pm, room, 119. Don't let anyone see you."

"I've got it," Marilyn said and then she was shocked and delighted it was D.H.

"Stephanie, how are you."

"I'm fine. I need to see you."

Marilyn now felt guilty. She had promised to keep in touch but had been so busy.

"I'm sorry that I haven't been over. I have been running like crazy."

"David's going to take advantage of this as long as he can. You need to give him an altimatime. Either he gets a replacement or you walk."

"You're right tomorrow I tell him one more week and that's it. Listen I'm on my way to an appointment. It shouldn't take long then I can come over."

"I need you to do something for me." Stephanie replied.

"No problem, I will be there in a little while, bye."

Marilyn looked at her watch.

"Were not going to make it are we."

"It can't be helped unless you don't mind breaking a few traffic laws."

"Go ahead."

In a few moments Marilyn was crunched down in the seat with her eyes closed as the driver almost sideswiped two cabs, ran through a yellow, and then a red light but they made it with exactly a minute to spare.

Marilyn was surprised when the car pulled up in front of an apartment. She checked the address again and it was correct. She pushed the intercom and was buzzed in. In side of the apartment it took a couple of moments for eyes to adjust to the darkness then she saw her. She was completely naked.

"I hope you have several hours, I've drawn a bath."

"I sorry but I don't."

"Oh, I see. Well never mind then," she said and then walked over to a couch and put on the bathrobe that was there.

"You've changed the parameters of our business relationship."

Stephanie had told her many times, don't get emotionally involved with your clients and try to keep them from getting involved with you. Marilyn walked over and she turned her back to her. Marilyn sucked on her ear.

"If you give me more notice, I will come and spend the whole day with you or the whole night." Marilyn put her hand inside of her robe; she resisted but then relented when she started massaging her breast.

"I'm sorry if I snapped at you. I've been burning the candle at both ends," Marilyn said softly. Marilyn took off her robe, threw it to the side, and then she ran her hands all over her body.

"No, it's my fault. I should have asked you first."

Marilyn took off her trench coat and adjusted the dildo.

"Please make an appointment for all night. I would like that," Marilyn said as she pushed the dildo inside of her. "I know men who could do this for you."

"No, I like the way you touch me. You don't seem to find me repulsive."

Marilyn massaged her inner thighs and then her breasts and nipples.

"Is it because you fee sorry for me?"

"No, it's because you deserve it."

Marilyn then took her quick and hard.

The driver pulled up in front of a book store, Marilyn jumped out and didn't even notice the book signing notice on the door. She was feeling guilty about Stephanie again. She asked the clerk if there was a baby section. There were several rows of books. She had no idea there were so many books on having a baby. She found one titled 'My first Baby.' and thought it would be perfect, and 'What Every New Mother Should Know.' She found herself very near the book signing table and when the author took the book to sign and started talking Marilyn thought his voice was very familiar. In a few moments she was standing there staring at him and listening. He was about the right build and the more he talked the more she was convinced but, of course, she would have to see him totally naked to be sure. She grabbed one of his books Big Rupert: Far from Home. She looked at it while she stood in line. It was about a big St. Bernard with magical powers. It was a story about how to find your way home if you are lost. The author's name Charley Walters and a picture was on the back. When it was her turn he looked right at her.

"Who would you like to have it made out to?"

"Could you make it out to Stephanie, she is having her first baby."

"I hope they both enjoy it."

There was absolutely no recognition of her, no hesitation, no nervousness, just another woman in line but Marilyn looked closely at his hands and ears and was convinced.

On the way to Stephanie's she was wondering how she was going to tell her but then realized she didn't have to when she saw several Big Rupert books on her coffee table.

Stephanie sat on the couch.

"You are getting really big. How do you feel?"

"I feel fine except by body is going through all kinds of changes. They say having a baby is a natural thing but I don't know if it's natural for this body."

Marilyn showed her the baby books but kept the Big Rupert book in the bag.

"I didn't think to go get any books," Stephanie said. "I need a real big favor."

"Of course, anything I can do."

Stephanie was wearing a one piece maternity dress that came down to her mid thigh.

"I need you to do me."

"What?"

"I am absolutely horny and I need you," Stephanie pleaded and then she slid the top of her dress down over her breasts.

"You're just huge."

"I know; now I have big ones. They just ache."

Stephanie pulled back the breast, exposing the nipple, and Marilyn took it in her mouth.

"Oh, yes. They just ache to be sucked."

Marilyn sucked on one then the other and then massaged them as she rubbed her big stomach. Stephanie was in a trance and all she could do was moan. Marilyn put her hands between her legs.

"You're drenched down there."

"I know. It's been that way for days."

"Are you sure it won't hurt the baby."

"No, I checked. You can do it safely up until the eight month."

"Ok then lets get you into the bedroom."

Stephanie arraigned the pillows on the bed so she was half sitting up.

Marilyn took off her trench coat and showing the latex panties.

"I'm sure glad you come prepared."

Marilyn went into the bathroom and washed the dildo thoroughly and when she came out Stephanie was massaging her tits and tweaking her nipples.

"I can't wait to start breast feeding; I just know I'm going to come like crazy."

Marilyn got between her legs. She ran the dildo up and down her slit getting it nice and wet.

"Will you quite teasing me and ram it in."

Marilyn pushed all of it inside of her in one steady motion.

"Oh, yes, I need it so bad. I miss having orgasms every day."

"I thought you were just supposed to please the client," Marilyn said as she worked the dildo in and out and from side to side.

"Oh, that's a job perk honey. Don't you have incredible orgasms when you service them?"

"Yes, but I was feeling guilty about it."

"Never feel guilty, why do it if you don't get off on it. Now do me really hard."

"Are you sure? Either do me hard or do me for hours, it's your chose."

Marilyn grabbed the headboard.

"Do you do Leslie good and hard?"

"Yes, I do her until she screams."

"What a lucky woman. I want to scream."

Marilyn used her powerful frame to plow into her until she screamed out her orgasm. Stephanie got on her hands and knees and Marilyn drove it up hard from behind and massaged her tits until she could feel little droplets of liquid coming out. The dildo pushed back into Marilyn and she kept doing Stephanie until she felt her own explosion.

Stephanie slept for over and hour and Marilyn waited for her in the living room. When she came into the living room Marilyn gave her the Big Rupert book.

"I got it signed for you."

"Where was he signing?" Stephanie asked.

"Down at Crossway Books. Maybe I should have had him sign it D.H."

Stephanie was silent and Marilyn knew by the look on her face.

"I don't know what you are talking about."

"Oh, come on, I know it's him. I could tell by the voice, his hands, and his ears."

Marilyn was silent for several moments and then figured it out.

"He's the father isn't he?"

"Oh, all right, it's him."

"You had me worried sick. I thought he was with the mob, or a hit man, or a CIA operative, or some big shot in the government. A children's book writer, I would have never guessed that."

"You can't tell anyone. He's married with six children. It would ruin his career."

"Of course, I wouldn't tell anyone. It's just that I thought if I didn't please him completely I would disappear one day. How did you find out it was him?"

"The same way you did. I saw him on a talk show promoting one of his new books and I knew it was him right away. Who better to father my child than someone who writes children's books? He had his six kids on the show and they seemed normal and healthy."

"So, you asked him to be the father."

"Actually I black mailed him."

"You're not serious."

"I told him if he didn't get me pregnant I would go public about his sexual behavior. I stopped taking money from him months ago. That's why I was so surprised he gave me that check."

"I am seeing him in a few hours. Is there anything you want me to tell him?"

"Tell him that I'm well and very happy."

As the car made its way on to the freeway, Marilyn noticed the driver was looking at her in the rear view mirror; he always did when she changed clothes in the car. Sometimes she would give him a little show and hoping that they would not get into an accident. She wondered why he never asked for anything and wondered if he thought what she did was disgusting.

Marilyn put on the fish net stockings and changed into the black corset and then touched up her makeup.

Her cell phone rang.

"Marilyn?"

"Yes," she replied not recognizing the voice on the other end.

"It's Mackensie Taylor. You sure are a hard woman to track down. I'm in here in town for a few weeks working on Broadway. I sure would like to see you."

"If you want my services it's going to cost you."

"Any thing you want dear."

Marilyn couldn't help but smile.

"Just give me the time and place."

The driver found the back entrance to the hotel. He drove into the parking ramp and then out, made a circle of the block and then came back and double parked down the street. He checked up and down the street.

"We're clear."

"Ok, I'm ready."

He drove quickly up to the back entrance; she jumped out quickly and got the large suitcase she now called the portable torture chamber out of the trunk. Marilyn got out wearing a large hat, sunglasses, and a trench coat, felling like a spy again. She went in the back entrance and went to the gift shop and at the same time checking the lobby for anyone that might appear to be working for the tabloids, bought a magazine, paid cash, to avoid a paper trail, made it look like she was reading it until no one was waiting for the elevator and then made her move. She kept looking at the magazine in the elevator, trying to hide her face, assuming there was a surveillance camera.

She looked up and down the hallway. It was clear. She knocked on the door. Inside the black-out curtains were pulled.

"This is the only hotel in the city that doesn't have surveillance cameras in the hallways," he said as he sat on the edge of the bed. He was totally naked except for the black, latex hood. Marilyn stripped off her outer garments with out saying a word. She set up the suite case and pushed up the bar. She took off her flat shoes and put on the six inch, spiked heels.

She came over, straddled him and pushed him down on the bed. She rubbed herself all over his face until the hood was all wet.

"My boy has been bad hasn't he?"

She grabbed his hand, he resisted, but she pulled him and restrained him with the leather cuffs. She raked his front and back with her fingernails but she was careful not to leave any marks. She brought out the riding crop and playfully swatted him on the front and back. Then she put on the nipples clamps.

"Present yourself, like I showed you."

He grabbed the bar and pushed out his ass giving her full access.

She whipped him several times and then ran the handle between his cheeks.

"This is supposed to be your punishment but I think you like it too much."

She spread his cheeks and ran her tongue up and down between them. She tried to push her tongue inside of him and he moaned his pleasure. She abruptly stopped and brought the ridding crop hard across his ass.

She reached around and found him totally hard.

"You like it way too much."

She got a leather harness out of the suite case. She ran the leather strap up and around the back of his neck, inserting the strap through the metal loop and then synched him up. He grunted and she pulled harder.

"Oh, please stop," he pleaded.

She kissed him forcing her tongue down his throat.

"Oh baby, I'm just getting started." She kissed his sack and tip as she pulled down on the strap, alternating the pleasure and pain until he erupted. She took off the nipple clamps and sucked on his sore nipples.

"I didn't tell you it was alright to come. Now I really have to punish you."

She drove the dildo deep inside of him and then pumped it in and out as she pulled on the leather strap until he was begging for another release. She took off the harness, released him, and then pushed him down on the bed. She guided his shaft between her cheeks and he moaned as she let it all go inside of her. She moved up and down and side to side and in a few moments felt him enlarge and then warm fluid inside of her. She found her spot and in a few seconds her body shook. She rubbed her juice all over his chest and then got off. He curled up into a fetal position.

"This so much better, now I can sleep."

"Sleep my little baby," she said as she massaged him. She got up and picked up the envelope on the dresser and counted ten one hundred dollar bills. She put two bills in her bra for the driver, three in her purse for Stephanie's baby and the rest inside her panties. She went into the bathroom and removed all her make up and brushed down her hair.

When she got to work, Jimmy and Mary were in the dressing room. Mary was naked except for a pair of chaps, a cow boy hat, and she was trying to squeeze into a small leather vest.

"So, what do we have today, Jimmy."

"You have white whale in an hour then housewife, gimpy, and then big guy."

Marilyn grabbed a couple of wet wipes and wiped between her legs. She turned in the chair so Jimmy could see everything and he stood there and watched as she wiped down her inner thighs.

David came in with a blond woman in tow. "This is Sheila. I told you I would find you some help."

Finally my replacement, Marilyn thought. She was five eleven. Her blond hair had a butch cut. She was wearing a baggy pair of sweat pants and sweat shirt.

"She won the state body building championship twice. Go ahead and show her."

Marilyn tried to hide her excitement as she removed her sweat pants and top. She was wearing a thong. She really didn't need a bra because her chest was all muscle but her nipples were hidden with a training bra. She took up a body building pose and they both inspected her.

"How about, Shelia the she devil?"

You are so hot, Marilyn thought as she looked through the rack of clothes and then handed her a leather thong and bra. She found two leather straps to highlight her powerful arms.

"I'm thinking Shelia the barbarian, no make up, just a wild untamed look."

"Very good, David responded. Well, train her in. Come on Jimmy."

Marilyn gave her a good looking over.

"Have you ever dominated someone sexually?"

"Yes,"

"And did you enjoy it."

"Yes,"

"Do you prefer men or woman?"

"I prefer woman but I like to dominate men."

Marilyn circled her and then touched her powerful thighs.

"Well it's not about your pleasure, its all about pleasing the client."

Marilyn went behind her and grabbed her large ass. It was hard as a rock.

"Your ass is magnificent."

"Thank you. Yours is not bad either."

"It's soft and flabby."

"I like a woman with a large, soft ass."

Marilyn reached around and felt her powerful chest and washboard stomach.

"Why do you want this job?"

"I can work here and still work on my body building. I figure it will pay better and be more fun than working in a convience store or a fast food place."

Marilyn rubbed herself on her rock, hard ass and then whispered into her ear, "I think I'm going to enjoy training you in." And Marilyn thought she was especially going to like doing that rock hard ass, spreading those powerful cheeks, tasting her flesh, and driving her tongue deep inside of her.

On the way home Marilyn figured she could steal white whale from David. She had DH, Uptown woman and Mckensie. They would be enough to start with. It was two in the morning and she was exshasuted. Her arms and shoulders were sore. She flopped on the couch and kidded off her shoes. A few moments Leslie came into the living room wearing a one piece pull over night gown that came down to mid thigh.

"I'm sorry that I woke you up."

"It's all right, I wanted to see you."

Marilyn could see the indentation of her nipple rings and chains in the thin material.

"I got my PhD and board certification today."

"That's fantastic."

"I have been looking at a building in Highland. I figure that I could be up and running in a month."

"Sounds wonderful David finally found a replacement."

"So are you going to quit right away?"

"Not for a couple of weeks. She's a real novice. She's going to need a lot of training." Her mind had been racing about all the things she wanted to do to her, with her.

Leslie slowly started to inch up her night gown.

"We are both going to very busy."

"Yes, very busy."

When she had the night gown all the way up, exposing her chains, she said, "Are you tired?"

"I'm very tired."

"That's too bad."

She started to let the night gown drop but Marilyn grabbed the chains and pulled her in close, tongued between her tits and then sucked on her nipples through the nipple rings, followed the chains down and then she reached between her legs. She pulled out the small vibrator that was inside of her.

"You are such a slut."

"I hope that I'm your slut?"

"Yes," Marilyn replied as she slipped two fingers inside of her and enjoying the feeling of her wetness.

"I do love you," Marilyn said.

"I love you too. Does that mean we are going to be together a long time?"

"Yes, a very long time."

"I will massage you. I saw your sister today" Leslie said as they made their way into the bedroom.

"Can you help her?"

"Of course, but she has a lot mental issues to deal with. She will be one of my first clients when I get my clinic open."

Leslie massaged her aching shoulders and arms and soon Marilyn was melting into the bed. She thought that she was too tired to be pleased but Leslie worked her magic and in a few moments she exploded inside.

Marilyn fell asleep. When she awoke she heard Leslie in the bathroom and she thought everything was perfect now. She got up and put on the strap on dildo and as soon as Leslie stepped out of the bathroom she grabbed her forcing her face down on the bed. She rammed the dildo into her from behind.

"Please don't," she pleaded.

"Please don't what?" Marilyn grunted as she rammed the dildo into as hard as she could.

"Please don't ever stop taking me."

"I don't plan too." Marilyn forced her up onto her hands and knees, rammed it in and out of her as hard and as fast as she could until she screamed out her orgasm and then they collapsed together on the bed, in each other arms, content and happy.

ABOUT THE AUTHOR

The author was born in Rockford, IL and after a stint in the military traveled extensively in the United States, Asia, and Europe. Then the author earned a degree in Liberal Arts from the University of Minnesota. The author is single and lives in Phoenix, Arizona.

www.ingramcontent.com/pod-product-compliance
Lightning Source LLC
Chambersburg PA
CBHW020240290526
45784CB00003B/1057